C000089178

REMEMBER, REMEMBER

Ed Cooke studied Psychology and Philosophy at Oxford University, graduating in 2004. In order to become a Grandmaster of Memory, he had to memorize 1,000 numbers in an hour, ten decks of cards in an hour (520 cards) and one deck in under two minutes. He was ranked seventh overall in the 2007 World Memory Championships, in which he has competed since 2003, and coached Josh Foer from novice to US Memory Champion in one year. As well as writing his weekly Mr Memory column in *The Times*, Ed teaches memory techniques and thinking skills around the UK. On most Sundays he can be found guiding memory walks around London.

REMEMBER, REMEMBER

LEARN THE STUFF YOU THOUGHT YOU NEVER COULD

ED COOKE

VIKING
an imprint of
PENGUIN BOOKS

VIKING

Published by the Penguin Group
Penguin Books Ltd, 80 Strand, London WC2R 0RL, England
Penguin Group (USA) Inc., 375 Hudson Street, New York, New York 10014, USA
Penguin Group (Canada), 90 Eglinton Avenue East, Suite 700, Toronto, Ontario,
Canada M4P 2Y3 (a division of Pearson Penguin Canada Inc.)
Penguin Ireland, 25 St Stephen's Green, Dublin 2, Ireland
(a division of Penguin Books Ltd)
Penguin Group (Australia), 250 Camberwell Road, Camberwell,
Victoria 3124, Australia
(a division of Pearson Australia Group Pty Ltd)
Penguin Books India Pvt Ltd, 11 Community Centre,
Panchsheel Park, New Delhi – 110 017, India
Penguin Group (NZ), 67 Apollo Drive, Rosedale, North Shore 0632, New Zealand
(a division of Pearson New Zealand Ltd)
Penguin Books (South Africa) (Pty) Ltd, 24 Sturdee Avenue, Rosebank,
Johannesburg 2196, South Africa
Penguin Books Ltd, Registered Offices: 80 Strand, London WC2R 0RL, England

www.penguin.com

First published 2008
1
Text copyright © Edward Cooke, 2008
Illustrations copyright © Yeti McCaldin, 2008

The moral right of the author has been asserted

Set in Berkeley Oldstyle Book
Book design by Janette Revill
Printed in Great Britain by Clays Ltd, St Ives plc

ISBN: 978–0–670–91785–3

www.greenpenguin.co.uk

Penguin Books is committed to a sustainable future
for our business, our readers and our planet.
The book in your hands is made from paper
certified by the Forest Stewardship Council.

To my wonderful sisters, Daisy, Eleanor, Florence and Phoebe

CONTENTS

INTRODUCTION

Read this book, and you'll be able to do some fun things.

You'll be able to recite all of our kings and queens in order, you'll be able to draw a freehand map of Europe, you'll be able to tell any interested parties how many presidents were called 'James' and you'll know which prime minister came before the Earl of Rosebery.

Indeed, you'll know that the Earl of Rosebery was a prime minister in the first place, and also that he married an heiress and won the Derby – like Edward VII, who, incidentally, was Queen Victoria's eldest son.

Knowing this kind of stuff is fun, it's useful and there is no need whatsoever for a gigantic brain.

If you're to believe me when I say this, and if you're to believe that by merely reading this book you'll know very many things, it may be helpful if I explain a little of how this project came about.

It began with something of a personal climb-down.

You see, for some years I'd been enjoying the social perks that come with being a 'Grandmaster of Memory': being ushered to the front of the queue at my local Tesco, receiving free bottles of champagne from unwary barmen, having my hands stroked by pretty girls with star-struck gazes.

These were obviously good times. But they were being generated by a terrible illusion. You see, my ability to learn a two-hundred digit number in the time it takes to feed a cat was causing people to overestimate the speed of my brain. People supposed that, since they could only manage about ten in a similar period, my brain travelled about twenty times faster than your standard road-going model.

Now, on numerous occasions I tried my best to explain that this was not the case. Repeatedly, I described the techniques that are entirely responsible for my capacity to remember: a wonderful collection of imaginative manoeuvres with a tradition of expert practice that stretches back millennia.

But mere explanation proved next to useless in defusing the aura of genius attached to my knowing, for instance, the address and phone number of every pizza-delivery joint in mainland Europe.

The core trouble was that you have to experience these techniques yourself before you can really trust them to work.

So I decided to actually *show* (forcefully, where necessary) my friends and family, and any members of the public who cared to take an interest, what was going on inside my head as I performed the memory marvels that were in danger of becoming the basis of my entire social life.

I therefore began a series of educative 'memory walks' in London. Ten or fifteen of us would gather of an afternoon at an appointed spot, on the understanding that if, after an hour or so, those present were not able to flawlessly recite both backwards and forwards the sixty or so kings and queens of England and Britain, or whatever else was on the menu for that week (giving relevant biographical details, of course), then I'd eat my hat.

We'd pick a path about some of the capital's landmarks and I'd instruct my fellow walkers to imagine bizarre scenarios – a bottle full of wolves at the foot of the National Portrait Gallery, a footballer in a toga against a lamp-post in

Hyde Park, bowtie-wearing geese escaping from a tub of lard in Little Venice. We proceeded at a lazy pace, and there was much good-humoured banter – along with the occasional high-five or boat ride.

These were memory techniques in action: ways of remembering that are kind on the mind, quickly learnt and formidably powerful. Invented by the Greeks, they were perfected in the Middle Ages and, though they still enjoy a mild renown, are ridiculously underused in the present day.

The results were most gratifying. People seemed to be enjoying themselves a good deal, and, more pertinently, I wasn't eating any hats. Recall was generally perfect, memories were still in place after many weeks and the facts learnt were regularly and effortlessly called to mind. Some of my walkers, it emerged, were even beginning to blaze ruinous trails through the pub quizzes of South London.

'This is really cool, Ed,' people told me. 'Can we learn the hundred most common varieties of cat next week?' I beamed as I nodded back at them, but behind this show of pleasure and pride a niggling cluster of doubts stopped me from wholeheartedly agreeing with them that this was indeed 'cool'.

I still privately suspected, you see, that all the things we were learning were things that normal people should know as a matter of course, that these walks were an embarrassing necessity, perhaps, for people like me who lack a thorough education, but were hardly something of general value.

This conviction lessened in power, though, as I noticed 'historians' joining my walks. At first I thought that there must be some mistake, or that they had come to mock me, but again and again I saw these 'scholars of history' at the back of my tour group, furtively forming the images as they followed along, all ears.

A thought as wonderful as it was appalling began to grow

in my mind. Maybe *no one* really knows this stuff; maybe even paid-up students of history go a bit blank when you start talking about the many sons of King Aethelwulf of Wessex.

Some amateur research was merited. A short investigation ensued. This is what was found:

- Oxford history undergraduates can freely name an average of only 9 of the 52 British prime ministers (that's 17%). They haven't even heard of more than half of them.
- Cambridge historians are even more ignorant.
- Their professors are not much better.
- The average pedestrian is on a yet more miserable footing.

I tried asking about our kings and queens. A slightly different, though equally bleak, picture emerged.

On hearing the combination of a common boy's name and a number – say, 'William' and 'the fifth' – people recognized that it was a king I was asking about, they 'remembered' he came from 'quite a while ago', they reported hearing something about him at some point, but were generally unable to provide any further detail. 'Was he the son of William IV?' some ventured. The objectivity required for my data gathering made it impossible for me to respond, 'No, you idiot.'

Such stumbling performances are totally justified for a king like William V, who never existed. But such responses, and there were many, are much less excellent when the man in question is a national hero, like Henry III.

Perhaps, though, I was being old fashioned. Perhaps knowing stuff is outdated. Maybe everyone has gleefully traded in their knowledge of the world for an internet connection and the capacity to bluff when the power is down.

When I asked people about this, though, they didn't seem to agree at all. They thought it would be a relief to know their kings and queens, for example, that it would be 'interesting' and 'helpful' and 'good'. Indeed, many reported the intention to learn them 'soon', which was encouraging, even if my follow-up test after six months revealed that none had.

So the situation seems to be this: hardly anyone knows this stuff yet a good deal of people would like to and that hardly anyone seems to know how to go about learning these things yet all are capable of doing so.

A simple and enjoyable means was needed by which anyone could remember a choice selection of things, things that everyone kind of wants to know but can't get to stick in their mind. So I wrote this book.

How this book works

Memory, you have to understand, works perfectly well in each of us – when it can be bothered.

The trick of remembering is to make sure your memory, a slothful creature prone to taking time out to do the mental equivalent of texting itself at the back of the class, sits up and takes notice.

The art of memory is thus the art of making sure that what you give your mind to remember is as bright and amusing and energetic and outrageous as possible.

Now, with this book, *Remember, Remember*, I've cooked up four stories that will, with luck, have your memory feasting like there's no tomorrow.

Gone are the bitterly boring long lists of names that your memory will have tried and failed to digest in the past. Instead, that same information has been hidden inside these four stories, four incident-packed romps – that have been designed to be gobbled up with the utmost ease.

The principle is that each name is transformed into a memorable event and that this list as a whole makes a string of events, or narrative.

To give one example: the eighth president of the US, Martin Van Buren, will become a Martian in a van that's burning. The thing about Martians in burning vans is that they're a lot more bright and amusing and energetic and outrageous than the sound of Martin Van Buren's name, making them about a hundred times easier to remember.

Every character will be transformed in similar fashion and, to remember their sequence, they'll be introduced in order along a familiar journey (in this case, through an airport as we head for our flight to the US).

Once you've read the story and want to recall a name or part of the sequence, you'll travel that route in your imagination – where you'll effortlessly find the things you saw happening there some time before. The name will spring automatically into your mind.

The sections on the prime ministers of Britain, the presidents of the US and the kings and queens of England and Britain each divide into two. The first half is the basic story of what happened: from this you'll learn to recite all the relevant people backwards as well as forwards, and you'll be able to jump in at any point and name the people either side.

The second section builds upon the first, touring over the same story, while adding historical and cultural colour. Here, you'll end up knowing something of the character of each leader, of their personal habits, their achievements and the events of their time. The second section thus adds depth and context to the first.

Ideally, you'll be inspired by the end to go it alone on any topic that interests you. And also to use the framework of

British and American history that this book provides, and take it in directions of your own.

The one rule of thumb that I might ask you to bear in mind as you read is simply this: if you imagine something vividly, you won't forget it.

With that, I'll leave you to your imaginative adventures.

KINGS AND QUEENS
OF BRITAIN AND ENGLAND

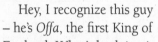

S PLAT!
Well, that's some way to
wake up in the morning! A
bellowing warlord has just
dumped a bucket of steaming
offal on my head!

Hey, I recognize this guy
– he's *Offa*, the first King of
England. What's *he* doing in my bedroom?

Oh, of course! We're meeting all the kings and queens
of England today. Offa is just the first of an extraordinary
collection, and we'll soon have the pleasure of meeting all
the others, one by one.

Come to think of it, we're due for a great day all round.
It's the last day of school – hurrah! – so lessons will be a
doss, and there's sports day in the afternoon . . . and then,
wonder of wonders, we've got months of summer holiday to
enjoy.

But this offal is spoiling the party a little. I mean, it's
running down into my pyjamas – *awful*! Let me just clear the
animal entrails *off o'* my face and check the time. The alarm
clock, this little *Merce*des car on the bedside table with the
time on its side, tells me it's 7.57 a.m.

So here are some things I didn't know until now – King

Offa is from the House of *Mercia* – and the *Merc* on the bedside table says he began his Mercian reign in AD 757.

Well, I think we can all agree that washing has just taken a flying jump to the top of our things-to-do list.

Follow me along this here landing to the bathroom. You don't mind me pointing out objects of interest, do you, as we go along? Take a look at the Wessex helicopter I've dangled up there on the ceiling. Doesn't it look like it's hovering? Magic, eh? No, no, there is actually a string, but it's so thin you can hardly see it.

It's there because this is the House of Wessex – except in my bedroom, of course, which is the House of Mercia. I've put these Wessexes up all over the place to remind me.

Come on, then – into the bathroom!

But fancy this – there's a massive blue boiled egg in the bathtub.

Breakfast in the bath? Not a bad plan.

SPLOTCH!

But not any more! The egg in the bath has just burst, spattering the whole bathroom with sticky tendrils of its hot liquid yolk. This really is revolting – it's gone everywhere, including my face, and I don't think it's even been cooked long enough to be safe to lick off. What a waste.

This *burst*ing *egg*, this *egg* that's just *burst*, is King *Eg-bert*. He's our second king.

Since the bathwater is now yellow, we'd better wash in the basin.

Unfortunately, a wolf's beaten us to it – I think we'd better wait our turn. An unusual character, this wolf is stuck in the neck of a large shampoo bottle, admiring himself in the mirror.

While he gets on with it, let me explain something.

Bottles mean *Aethels* in this household. When you see a bottle, you should be saying to yourself, 'We have an *Aethel* here.' You can think of *a full* bottle of *ethanol* to nail this association between bottles and *Aethels*.

So our *wolf* who's wedged in the top of a (shampoo) *bottle* is *Aethelwulf*, our next king.

But he's taking his time, isn't he? What a ponce! You'd think he was a teenage girl preparing for a prom the way he's carrying on.

He's making use of all three of the toiletries that this bathroom has got on offer. Mind you, I suppose it is his right; they are his sons, after all.

They're lined up on the little glass shelf beneath the mirror, each in a bottle of his own. The first bottle-son has a little bald man sticking out; the feathery head of a colourful bird peeks from the second; from the third, meanwhile, protrudes a tube of red lipstick.

Aethelwulf's grabbed hold of the biggest bottle now, the one with the bald man sticking out.

The *bottle* with the *baldy* is *Aethelbald*. Amazing: look how the wolf now puts his first-born Aethelbald to use as a roll-on deodorant, and how the perfectly spherical bald head spins in the bottle's casing as the wolf rolls it round his armpits.

Now he's grabbing the *bird* in the bottle, *Aethelbert*,

and passing him just beneath his nose. Listen to that high whirring sound as the bird busily sets to work, his beak a blur as he clips away at the wolf's moustache. He's quite a good barber, is Bert the bird, and the wolf is soon trimmed to perfection.

Now that he's deodorized with Aethelbald and shaved with Aethelbert, the bottled wolf takes hold of his final son, the bottle of lipstick. Goodness knows why but this wolf wishes to *redden* his lips. So he purses them as he applies a honking red sheen of *Aethelred*, taking care not to get any on his newly trimmed moustache.

At last the wolf's finished, and off he toddles, leaving the sink to us.

Let's quickly dash some water over our faces and clear away that offal and egg before getting downstairs for breakfast. It feels lovely, doesn't it, the cool, fresh water? And while we savour it let's run through our heads the various kings we've seen so far today:

After the Mercian King Offa, there've been five Wessex kings: King Egbert, bursting in the bath, followed by Aethelwulf and his three bottle sons. In order, those sons were: Aethelbald – the deodorizer, Aethelbert – the moustache-trimmer, and Aethelred – his lipstick.

We're fresh and clean now, and do you smell this? The godly scent of a fry-up is wafting through the bathroom door. Yum yum. I could use a decent feed – are you going to hang around here or follow me to that food?

But, oh my goodness! It's right here on the landing! The fry-up's being cooked on a fire on the carpet!

And there's the little hooligan responsible for all this, spatula in hand, looking like it's the most natural place in the world to cook breakfast! He's tending to his sausages and slapping down another rasher of bacon as we speak.

This outrageous *all-fried* breakfast man is *Al-fred* the

4

Great, and he is our next king (and Aethelwulf's fourth and final son to take the throne).

As we go past, he offers us some of his all-fried fare.

Yes, I know, it smells amazing, but we can't possibly accept – he'll be starting fires in our bed next. So let me just boot him out of the way, and we'll carry on heading downstairs to our cornflakes.

But what a palaver! Instead of soft carpet, look: the stairs are hidden beneath a frothy green torrent of elderflower cordial. How on earth are we supposed to get down to the kitchen now?

Wait a second – the answer's appeared in the form of a massive wooden head, of all things. It's jovially bouncing down these elderflower-cordial rapids, cool as a cucumber.

A wood-head is a wood-ed is an Ed-ward, obviously. This here wooden head in the elderflower cordial must be *Edward the Elder*, then – our next king.

If Edward the Elder can do it, so can we. With a bit of help. Go on! Grab hold of him! Keep clinging on now as we career down the stairs in these foaming elderflower waters.

5

But this isn't good: we're picking up speed, going too fast! We're going to be thrown out of the stream. Brace yourselves!

Wheee! Splat!

Well, that was a reasonably soft landing, all things considered. Luckily, we flew from the stream at the bottom of the stairs into two large bottles of fake tan. They saved our skin, no doubt about it. But what atrocious smell is this? Doesn't it make you want to retch?

This orange gunk, this tanning cream that's been spattered all over the walls and ceiling, pongs like nothing I've ever smelt before.

Bottles of tan? These must be *Aethels – tan*. King *Aethelstan* is our next Wessex king.

But let's not dawdle. Breakfast awaits!

Urgh! What *is* this? There I was: striding into the kitchen expecting cool, hard tiles beneath my feet, but instead there's something hot, wet and chunky seeping into my socks.

I've just walked straight into a mound of heads. And look! On top of the *head-mound*, there's *Ed-mund*! Far from apologizing, he asks me if I think his head-mound is magnificent.

Thinking about it, I probably do. But I'm not going to tell him that. So I tell him he's a disgrace, and skirt dismissively past Edmund the Magnificent (our next king) and his ill-placed head-mound.

Right, after all these upsets we need to focus on Operation Cornflakes. We need some milk.

The fridge is over there, but – uh-oh – it seems to be breaking down. It's making the sloshing sound you expect from washing machines.

Carefully now, let's open the door. KETCHUP! A slush of ketchup is gunking out of the fridge and on to the floor. Yoghurts, lettuces and lumps of cheese are being swept out by the flood. This is disastrous.

Open the door a bit more and you'll see who's responsible for this: there's a severed head, stained a bright red, surrounded by a lake of ketchup. And he's not finished yet. He's got a full bottle in his mouth and, drunk with glee, he's clamping his teeth down and squirting it all over the place.

This gleeful *head* that's *red* is King *Edred*, our next king.

The milk, meanwhile, is irretrievably lost, unless someone feels like digging around in this gunk? I thought not. We'll have our cornflakes dry, then. Wretched.

At least we can have them in a clean bowl, though. Did you hear that bleep? The dishwasher's just finished its cycle. Let's open it up.

Double wretchedness! As the steam clears, all there is to see is a young boy sporting a soggy *head-wig*. And the

liquid he's just been washed in is, by the smell of things, well . . . a most unappetizing one. I'm sorry to say this, but it's quite evident that his *head-wig* is wet with human urine.

King *Eadwig*, that's his name, appears to have wet himself during the wash, and has thus been doused in his own wee. It makes you want to sneeze.

7

It'll be no surprise to the reader to hear that King Eadwig's other name is King Edwy. He's the only king with two names in the directory, so to speak. Thank goodness.

No milk, no bowls. The cornflake plan's gone out the window. This is actually really annoying: today's a big day, and we'll be needing some fuel . . .

. . . and there I was complaining! What a fool I've been! Listen to this fizzing and spluttering sound coming from the oven! If I'm not mistaken, that is the sound of kippers being grilled in goose fat – my favourite meal.

Ouch! A double whammy! Opening the oven, a wave of heat smacks us in the face, followed soon after by the realization that the interior of our oven is a kipper-free zone.

Instead, there's a head in the orange light of the grill, calmly inspecting us as he puffs away on a fat Cuban cigar.

This is infuriating! We're supposed to be inspecting the food, not vice versa.

The *head* with a *cigar*, King *Edgar*, doesn't seem to care either about the social niceties or the fact that he's being cooked. He's just *sooo* peaceful.

He's Edgar the Peaceable, our next king.

Well, our breakfast plans have been royally scuppered, you've got to admit, but let's not panic. We can at least hydrate. All top athletes drink loads of water – maybe it'll help us run faster in sports day.

Here's a glass, a clean one, I think. We'll fill it up with cool water at the sink.

Hello? What's this? Oh heck, there's yet another severed head in here. This one must be wooden: he's bobbing up and down in the soapy waters.

8

And I think he's muttering at us . . . Yes, you can clearly hear him muttering insults! The cheek! He just called me a thieving bog-weasel! That's both unkind and untrue.

Now, I'm not normally quick to anger, but, when you can't get a glass of water from your own sink without abuse from some piece of wood, things have gone beyond a joke.

So now our glass is full – theeeeeere we go! – I'm going to make a martyr of our mutterer by blasting him with the hot tap.

No – no complaints – I won't have it. Ha! The deed is done!

Oh, and by the way: with this simple act of violence, we've made our next king, *Edward the Martyr*.

The trouble with all this is that water makes for a pretty poor breakfast. Yes, we're being hydrated, which is great, but, if it doesn't taste of anything, it's not breakfast.

At least this problem is easily solved: there on the kitchen table is a jumbo bottle of trusty Ribena.

The bottle of Ribena, full of its red liquid, combines being a bottle (an *Aethel*) with being *red*. It's therefore an *Aethelred*. Good morning, King Aethelred!

Don't mind us; we're just livening up our water with a bit of your nectar.

As we pour some of Aethelred into the water, however . . . what's going on? The water's turning green.

This isn't what we bargained for. Green is not red – in fact, it's most un-red.

This clearly isn't just any old

9

Aethelred, this is an *un-red* Aethelred. This is Aethelred the Unready.

Now you could say that our dietary preparations for sports day have left a lot to be desired. I mean, look what's happened! You just don't suffer these kinds of disturbances in the Olympic Village. And, no, I'm not making excuses; just consider the facts.

The landing was on fire, for a start. That was unsettling, even if it was just Alfred preparing his all-fried breakfast, and having to swim down those elderflower rapids with Edward the Elder, a wooden head, before cannoning at the bottom into Aethelstan, the two bottles of tanning-cream? The ones that stank? That's hardly choice preparation, is it?

And everything seems to be conspiring against us in the kitchen too. First, we trod in Edmund's mound of heads at the door. Then Edred denied us our milk because he was spurting so much ketchup in the fridge. And Eadwig, damp with his own Edwy in the dishwasher? Did Steve Redgrave have to deal with that kind of thing?

The oven, our next point of call, lacked any food, remember, because a head had decided he needed to smoke his cigar inside – that was Edgar – and we couldn't even get ourselves a drink without being hassled by a wooden head (Edward the mutterer, soon to become Martyr).

Finally, when all we asked for was a little taste of Aethelred's Ribena, even that failed to meet our expectations: it turned our breakfast green.

But do I expect these setbacks to derail our bid for glory? Not a bit of it! By hook or by crook, we'll get our carbohydrates somewhere.

We could investigate, for instance, down the back of the sofa in the sitting room, where Dad is forever losing half-eaten Danish pastries. So much so, indeed, that we've taken to calling the room the 'House of Denmark'. The sofa is now stickier than a fly-trap, of course, but we'll just look inside, and not sit in it.

Onwards to the House of Denmark, then!

By golly! You'll never guess who's on the sofa!

It's Sven-Göran Eriksson! Hallo *Sven*!

Sven tries to get up to greet us, but the poor fellow's stuck. All he can do is turn his head. And check this out – he has grown a *forked beard*! Perhaps he's trying to disguise himself after those dismal World Cup showings. Or perhaps the reason he's sitting there with a forked beard is that he's our next king, *Sweyn Forkbeard*.

Despite sitting on a goldmine of Danish pastries, Sweyn's chosen something rather different to eat. By his feet, on a small stool, Sweyn has stacked himself a mound of those gruesome heads we nearly tripped over on the way into the Wessex kitchen – something to snack on while he watches TV. He's not gone for a magnificent configuration, you'll notice, but he's stacked them very safely all the same, having secured the structure with some iron that's holding in the head-mound's sides. Well, this must be why this stack of heads is called *Edmund Ironside*, the next in the line of England's rulers.

We should be off to school soon, but while we're here we may as well spare a couple of minutes to catch some telly. Let's see what's on.

Well, get this. What's literally on the TV is a great big canoe – it positively dwarfs the set beneath it. This *canoe* represents *Canute the Great*, our third sitting-room king.

11

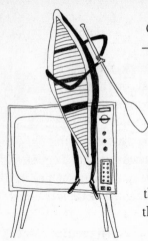

On screen now – brilliant!
– there's an episode of *Neighbours*
airing. And it gets better – more
or less everyone's favourite
Neighbours' character, *Harold*,
seems to be the hero of the bit
we've happened to catch.

Look at him, the poor chap.
He's stuck out in the middle of
the river, trying to summon up
the courage to swim ashore.

He's dithering as only Harold
can dither: maybe the waters are
too cold for his liking.
Watch as he dips a foot in
to test them, only to whip
it back out with a pained
sigh.

And, blimey, look at
those feet of his! To think
that I nearly missed them!
They're just horrible
– they're covered entirely
in a thick matting of grey hair.

So one thing's clear: this is *Harold Hairy-feet*, or, rather,
Harefoot that we're watching on TV. *Harold Harefoot* is our
next king.

But Harold has now got company; this looks interesting. A
small watercraft, perhaps a canoe, is bouncing along the river
towards him at great speed, sometimes almost doing the
water-going equivalent of a wheelie.

And now we can see why! The whole front portion of,
yes it's a canoe, is not there; it's obviously been chopped off.
Whoever this is out on the river is riding in only *half a canoe*.

12

And he's headed straight for Harold. There's going to be a collision. It's difficult to see how both of them can come out of this in one piece.

With a terrible crash, *half a canoe* smashes into Harold, who disappears with a terrific groan into the waters. Poor Harold! I hope he's OK . . .

Half a canoe is our next king, King *Harthacanute*.

'Neeighhhhhhhhhhhhbours, everybody . . .' That's the end of the episode, then. Too bad, I was enjoying myself.

The House of Denmark's been pretty happening, eh? Sweyn Forkbeard on the sofa with our second head-mound, Edmund Ironside, at his feet. Canute the Great's canoe on top of the telly. Harold Harefoot getting knocked off the throne by Harthacanute . . . You can't argue with that.

Now, then, shouldn't we be thinking about heading –
SMASH!

Weeeooo-weeeooo-weeeooo . . .

Breaking glass, the car alarm . . .
Holy smoke – I think someone's nicking our car!

Stop them!

We bound from the House of Denmark and out of the front door to save the family wheels. But what a sight greets our eyes! There are no thieves here, only a massive wooden head.

A wooden head that's crushed our car almost flat! Look at the thing; that head must have been dropped from a considerable height.

It doesn't take a detective to find the culprit for this one.

There he is, hovering guiltily away in a Wessex helicopter fifty yards above the car.

'You imbecile!' we cry at the helicopter pilot. 'You miserable, pathetic Anglo-Saxon imbecile!'

Instead of the pilot, though, it's the car-crushing head of wood who responds: 'Sorry, sorry,' he says. 'I confess – it's all my fault.'

'Are you sure?'

'Of course I'm bloomin' sure,' the head snaps back. 'Just accept my confession. I'll sort out the insurance.' At that, the head shuts up.

This *confessing head-wood* is *Edward the Confessor*, and the helicopter hovering away above reminds us we're back with the House of Wessex.

Right, well, thanks to our Edward, we're going to need a new way to get to school. It'll have to be the bus. Luckily, there's a stop just down the street.

Let's head for that bus stop, passing the squashed car and leaving through the garden gate – which someone's helpfully holding open for us. You'll never guess who.

Amazingly, it's Harold from *Neighbours* again! 'Hello again, *Harold*,' we say, carefully eyeing his feet. But there's no hair. His feet are undeniably, disgustingly bald. And he is tapping one impatiently on the dewy grass. We take the hint, thank him for his kindness and head off, still trying to come to terms with this being an entirely different Harold. *Harold II*, indeed, the last of the kings of Wessex – the last of the Anglo-Saxons.

We're now on Norman Street, headed for the bus stop a few yards distant.

Up close, this stop turns out to be one of the most

14

nondescript, utterly run-of-the-mill bus stops you've ever seen. It's almost aggressively *normal*, which tells us we're at the point where the House of Normandy begins.

All things considered, it's hardly surprising that the billy goat in front of us is trying to destroy the side of the stop with a rock-hard conker. It needs some kind of improvement, and why not cosmetic dentistry? The goat is making the dents by swinging the conker on a string between his teeth. Fantastic technique, but do pipe down, Billy – you're in a public place.

While we wait for the bus I'm going to start stretching my hamstrings, bending down like this. Nothing like warming up in good time.

As I do so let me explain something about **billy goats**. They stand for **Williams**. Bill is a nickname for 'William', you see, so when you see a billy goat, you must say to yourself, 'Aha! We have a William on our hands.'

This first *billy* goat (the one we just saw with his *conker*) is, then, *William I the Conqueror*, the first Norman king.

My next stretch requires a sitting position, so let's move under the shelter.

Oh – but the bench is taken . . .

No worries, though. I mean – is this not the cutest thing you ever saw? A little red-haired billy goat is curled up under a rug on the bench, shivering. The poor thing doesn't have a home.

He is called *Billy Roofless* by his pals, but to us he'll always be *King William II 'Rufus'*.

Aha! There's our bus – that very normal-looking one pulling in now.

With a hiss and a clunk, the doors slide open. An enormous white chick is the first to hop aboard, waddling up the steps.

Now this is important, so listen up. There are eight Henries in this monarchy of ours, and each will be a different kind of *hen*, or bird. So remember this: **hen** (or **bird**) = **Henry**.

This first hen, this twittering outsize chick who's now buying his ticket, is *Henry I*.

As our first Henry waddles on to the bus, the bus driver comes in to view: it's Stephen Fry. How cool is that? If I'd known that one of Britain's national treasures drove the school bus every day, I would have given up on the car ages ago. What Stephen Fry is doing driving buses is anyone's guess, but it is, I suppose, convenient: King *Stephen* is our next king.

We're about to follow Henry I on to the bus and meet our hero driver when, with a terrible bash, a van rams into the side of the bus.

A moment later, a woman with a scraggy old mat in her hand leaps out to attack. This *mat-hold*ing maniac, *Mat-ilda*, obviously doesn't do road rage by halves.

Having bludgeoned her way through the window, she sets

16

about whacking Stephen repeatedly over the head. Stephen's trying to protect himself, but it's all so sudden, so vicious! Why on earth is she being so mean?

Matilda is conducting a (drive-by) mat-press: an *m-press* for short. This is a technique of persuasion, you may know, where you hit someone so hard over the head with a mat that they do whatever you say.

Aha – so the mat-holder, Matilda, is an *empress* on a mission to persuade. Her full name is *Empress Matilda*. And her mission? Well, listen to what she's bellowing, one word at a time, in between whacks of the mat!

She – wants – her – son – to – be – bus – driver.

Yes, I agree, this is an amusing spectacle, but I've had enough of it, to be honest. Did you know that if we're late for registration, we won't get to compete in the afternoon sports? If Matilda hadn't turned up, we'd probably already be at school by now.

Finally, Stephen gives in to Empress Matilda's m-press and turns off the bus engine. The son can drive, but the bus stays here.

With the Norman bus out of service, it looks like we're going to have to pile into angry Matilda's van, her *anger-van*, and be driven to school by her son instead.

But what fun it turns out to be! Our driver is a hen. A *hen* with *two* squawking heads.

A two-headed hen like this has to be *Henry II*. He's the first king of the royal House of *Angevin*.

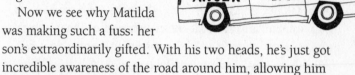

Now we see why Matilda was making such a fuss: her son's extraordinarily gifted. With his two heads, he's just got incredible awareness of the road around him, allowing him to take what seem to be enormous risks.

It's an education watching him operate: one moment he's checking both side mirrors simultaneously, the next he's searching, with one head, for a map in the glove compartment while he concentrates on honking the horn with the other.

At this rate we'll be at school in record time!

But the van's pretty packed, and Henry II pops one head round to say he wants a few of us out on the roof.

No problem, driver! Up through the sunroof we climb, joining a couple of other passengers in the wind. And fancy this – we recognize them both!

At the front I do believe that's Richard Branson who's just sat down above the driver with a jousting pole to hand and his feet hanging down on the windscreen. He's a famously brilliant jouster, is *Richard*, and he's obviously come up here to hone his skills.

As we wing through the traffic, he's knocking innocent people off their bikes with sharp thrusts of his pole. A young cyclist has just gone cartwheeling clean over our heads!

What striking bravery – what a *lion's heart* – this first Richard (*Richard I 'the Lionheart'*) is showing here as he jousts away.

Right on the back of the bus, meanwhile, is one of our rivals for the fastest person in school: John Travolta. He's toned and honed to perfection – look at the moves he's throwing on his flashing dance floor! He's like greased lightning, this guy, and now he's doing some relatively hardcore stretches, probably to try to intimidate us – get a load of those splits! Ouch!

Our first John, Travolta, reminds us that *King John* is the king after Richard the Lionheart.

18

Whoooa! The bus has just screeched to a halt by the school gates and John, not expecting the change in pace, has gone toppling off the anger-van roof on to the pavement below.

So that, then, is the end of the royal House of Angevin.

That was pretty intense, eh? Let's take a moment, shall we, to steady our nerves with a quick recap.

Working backwards from the anger-van, the House of Angevin, we had King John (Travolta) and King Richard (Branson) being driven by our two-headed Henry II.

Before that we were among the Normans where Empress Matilda was battering Stephen the bus driver, from whom the fluffy white chicklet Henry I was trying to buy a bus ticket.

Underneath the bus shelter, we met the cute roofless billy goat (that was William II 'Rufus') and outside the bus shelter William the Conqueror, the first billy goat, was whacking away with his conker.

Good. So, bring your minds back here to the school entrance – and enjoy the view!

It's a vast pagoda towering over formidable iron gates, glorious in its intricate detailing and decoration.

The architecture is marred only by that straggly bundle hanging from the gates, swinging back and forth in the morning breeze. I hope there's good reason why this ugly *net* full of *aged plants* is spoiling the scene.

Actually, as excuses go, this isn't bad. It's there to tell us that we've reached the *plant-age-net,* or *Plantagenet,* era of monarchs.

Let's head into the playground. Watch out, though, for this peacock at the gate. He's the sentry and a bit of an unpredictable old bird, as likely to wish you a cheery good morning as bite your head off for having your shirt untucked.

'Morning, sir!'

'Morning!'

Now we're safely through, turn round and get a good look at the three insanely lifelike eyes on his tail-feathers. Can you believe those aren't real? From here it's like they're following your every step, not missing a thing. Sends shivers down my spine.

Anyhow, this *hen* with *three* eyes in his tail is called *Henry III*, he's our third bird.

We're all the way into the Plantagenet playground now, and you've got to say that there's a festival atmosphere today. There's all sorts going on, even live music – which sounds awesome, actually. That's some serious volume! Let's check it out.

Bumbling across, we can make out three musicians jamming away in the bike shed.

Each of the three is an Ed playing a wooden instrument. Musical Ed-woods.

In all, there are eight such post-Norman musical Edwards, identified by the different kinds of wooden musical instrument they play. Basically, wherever there's a **wooden instrument** there's also an **Edward**. And, since each Ed has a different instrument, no two Eds will be exactly the same.

Well . . . that's not to say they won't look similar. But that's because we could only find one Ed to model for our illustrator, who needed to know what Eds look like. I was in the office at the time and was reluctantly persuaded to pose. So all Edwards from now on in will be playing a wooden instrument and they'll look remarkably like, er, me.

Listen up, folks – the band has begun to play again.

Ed I, on the left, begins the number, hammering down hard with a *boom! boom! boom!* on the bass drum. You can feel it in your bowels. Great power from *Ed I*.

Now it's *boom patter patter patter boom patter patter* as *Ed II* adds the quicker beat of his bongos to Ed I's bass. Wonderful to hear Ed II, in the middle, on his bongos!

And a big hello to *Eddie III*, the star of the show! He's on the right and has just come in with a thunderous droning noise, achieved by playing on three didgeridoos simultaneously.

Look at this special breathing technique he's using: his cheeks are puffing in and out like the pistons of a steam engine. And the sound he makes – an atrocious racket – wakes up reptilian feelings in your brain. Not for the faint-hearted.

Anyhow, as we look at the three Eds, from left to right we see Edward I with his bass drum, Ed II with his bongos and Ed III blowing his three didgeridoos.

They finish their piece, and the audience bursts into wild applause. Admittedly the audience consists only of Richard and Judy, who are filming live today from the Plantagenet playground. But they're over the moon with the performance, jumping up and down on their sofa shouting, 'Encore!' again and again.

Richard's obviously another King Richard. That he is never seen without his partner, Judy, indicates that he is *Richard II* – there are always, in effect, two of him.

So Richard and Judy, applauding Eds I, II and III, are Richard II.

We have to leave before the next number because the class register's about to begin, and this is, as I said earlier, the one day of the year we don't want to be late (for fear of getting banned from sports day).

But what a hullabaloo greets us as we walk into the classroom! It's as if we've just walked into a henhouse and been mistaken for a snarling fox: there's the most appalling squawking, birds are flying in all directions and a dense spray of bird feed fills the air.

The walls, meanwhile, are covered in the long and lanky red roses of Lancaster, this being the henhouse of Lancaster.

Only the arrival of the teacher calms things down. And who wouldn't be scared of this thing? He's possibly the largest living teacher I've ever seen, and easily the largest bird. A turkey of epic proportions, he must weigh at least four tons. You can see ripples shuddering through the fat beneath his feathers as he treads into the room.

Our *fourth bird*, this four-ton turkey, is *Henry IV* – and he has four woggles, lest we forget it.

Now things have settled down, we can get a better look at the classroom layout. Very unconventional: there are just five desks in this rosy room and they've been arranged in V-formation, with the point at the front.

As the register proceeds, five peregrine falcons swoop one by one with bloodcurdling affirmative caws to take up their desktop perches. Look at these muscular birds of prey: are they not the most perfect birds of war you ever saw?

It would be appropriate if they were, because these falcons arranged in V-formation represent our most warlike king, King *Henry V*.

Every classroom has its rebels. In this case, the rebels are six penguins, fooling around at the back.

Watch them as they blatantly disobey school rules by eating in class. They're devouring a six-pack of Penguin biscuits. Isn't it gorgeous how they throw their heads back, shaking a Penguin each down their throats? And what a sound they make as they do so – as if they're gargling gravel.

The turkey looks pretty displeased, but there's nothing he can do about it: lads will be lads, after all. These six represent *Henry VI*.

At the end of the register, the turkey sums up what the day holds. Our only lessons, beginning in a few minutes, will be double science; then it's lunch. And lunch will be followed, of course, by what

we're all looking forward to: sports day in the afternoon.

So in the House of Lancaster, a great red-rose-lined henhouse, we've had Henries IV, V and VI. Henry IV was a four-ton turkey doing the register, Henry V was five falcons sitting in V-formation and at the back we had Henry VI, our collection of rebellious biscuit-eating penguins.

Science is in five minutes, and the penguins are already headed that way. So follow me down this corridor and up these . . . dear heaven! Climbing these stairs is going to be difficult. They're covered in a great tangle of thorny white roses. These roses have got to be the white roses of York.

Everyone's a bit unsure how to deal with this situation.

At least someone's taken the initiative, though, as we all stand there gawping. A guy's whipped out a four-stringed bass guitar and he's playing a few tunes to keep us entertained while we climb carefully up.

Why, it's none other than *Edward IV*, plucking away with the four fingers of his right hand! He's pumping out a few funky riffs – I think this one's the fourth – from the bottom steps of the stairs. Listen to him go!

Behind him, a little up the stairs, can you spot the cheeky junior-school boy pretending he's part of Ed IV's band? He's playing along air-guitar fashion on a little size-five cricket bat.

He's got all the basics sorted, this youngster, if you look at the way he strums the blade and dances his fingers over the splice (the point on the bat where the handle meets the blade,

24

making a V-shape in the wood). *Edward V* this is, then, joining Ed IV's music-making on the stairs.

Ho ho – who's this sinister-looking creature at the top of the stairs, silhouetted against the white double doors of the science labs?

Whoever he is, he's had a third leg fitted between the normal pair, and he's practising running around. Extremely badly, I might add.

You know what? I recognize this guy – it's Ricky Gervaise off the telly – seriously practising for the three-legged race by himself! What a nonce!

Our third *Ricky*, with his *three legs*, represents King *Richard III*.

So on these stairs, the House of York, we've had Edwards IV and V and Richard III.

We walk past Ricky through the double doors into science. These doors, by the way, are the reason the whole lab is known as *Two-doors*: as the royal House of Tudor.

The Tudor science room is divided into two: at the front is the classroom proper; behind it, the lab tables where we do the experiments.

What have we got to look forward to today, I wonder? Well, as always, it'll be one lesson of theory and one of experiments.

Theory's never that fun, but at least we have an awe-inspiring golden eagle for a science teacher. Here he is at the front, spreading his wings to silence the class.

They never fail to hypnotize us with their incredible *seven-foot span*, and we fall silent obediently.

He's getting on with the lesson now, using a projector to show all seven of the topics he's prepared for today's lesson on the board. Groan. He seems to think we're here to learn on the last day of term. But if that's what is wanted by *Henry VII*, our seventh bird and first Tudor king, then we'll just have to sit through it.

As usual, the teacher's pet, an *eight-foot* ostrich, is answering all the questions at the front of the class. Look at him, trying to stick his rubbish ostrich wing up in the air to catch the teacher's attention. Our largest bird, he's our last Henry. *Henry VIII*.

And that completes the set of Henries! Let's reminisce a second.

To begin with, we had a fluffy white chick, Henry I, climbing on to the school bus. The replacement bus driver in the anger-van was Henry II, the two-headed hen. He raced us to the school gates, where we had our uniforms inspected by the peacock, Henry III.

The following three Henries were all present in our classroom for morning registration. There was Henry IV – the turkey doing the register, our other classmates – the five falcons of Henry V and then the six Penguin-eating penguins of Henry VI, who were huddled together at the back.

Now we've just completed the set with Henry VII, our awesome eagle of a science teacher, and the eight-foot ostrich Henry VIII, his favourite pupil.

We'll obviously take up position at the back, well out of the way of the action, to slack away till the end of the lesson.

I must say, meanwhile, that I'm beginning to get a bit

nervous about this afternoon's sports. I really should be warming up – it's not that long till it all begins.

What I need is a bit of light aerobic work.

And listen to this – the perfect opportunity has presented itself: one of the littlest kids with us in the back row has just piped up on his little recorder, jigging as he plays. Why not get the blood flowing with a few quiet dance moves here at the back?

The kid taps his fingers merrily over the six-holed instrument, and the majority of the class begins to bop up and down to his tune. Unfortunately, by the sixth number, he's a bit exhausted, our piper, and keels over dead.

He's Edward VI, the sickly musical child king.

Never mind! The bell's gone, and now we get to do experiments. Any experiment we like, in fact, because it's the last day of term.

Let's see what everyone's gone for!

On the near edge of the table closest to us, Jane is being as boring as ever and is 'experimenting with a new blend of tea'. When you could be throwing potassium into swimming pools and causing explosions, there's really no excuse for such a choice of investigation. And we tell her this.

But she's unrepentant: she wants to show us that 'there's more to life than PG Tips' by having us taste her 'Lady Grey' tea.

What is Lady Jane Grey *like*?

Forget it – look at Mary on the other side. She's much feistier, and is taking full advantage of 'open lab'. She's the blood-spattered girl over there with the lamb bleating under her arm, a bit of a character.

27

The class joke is that Mary has a little lamb . . . with mint sauce . . . for breakfast, lunch and tea.

Today she is experimenting on a new recipe for the famous bloody Mary cocktail. She's seeing how it tastes with lamb's blood in.

But, urgh, that's not nice. I'm not even going to explain what she's done now – just know that after *Lady Jane Grey*, Bloody *Mary I* is our next monarch, and if you farm sheep, you should not invite her to stay during lambing season.

We'll move on to the third experiment, taking place on the table at the back of the classroom. The school beauty, an absolute dead-ringer for Cate Blanchett, is busying herself with her lizards. She is putting them to bed after a hard spell of rehearsals.

Is it possible to train lizards to perform a play? In this beauty's capable hands, it is.

This Cate Blanchett lookalike we find putting *lizards to bed* at the back of the labs is Queen *Elizabeth* I. And what a coincidence that Cate Blanchett will one day play the lead in the movie of the life of Elizabeth I!

The bell goes and double science is over – hurrah! The experiments, conducted by Lady Jane Grey, Bloody Mary I and Elizabeth I, are complete. It's time we left the Tudors and got some lunch. And goodness we're hungry – to think we've not eaten so far today.

The dining hall isn't much to look at: a food counter manned by a couple of chefs runs along the right-hand wall of the narrow room, and all the seating's outside, beyond the far end over there in the fresh air.

Today, of course, there's stew on the menu. That's the way it goes here. They've turned the task of making stews from any and every ingredient into an art-form – that's why we call this place the 'House of Stew-art'. For some reason, though, they spell it oddly, with a 'u' – perhaps you noticed the word 'STUART' emblazoned above the doors as you came in.

Sliding our tray along the runner here, we reach the first chef. What a legend he is! How many schools can boast Sean Connery in the kitchen? I mean – the very first James Bond!

Would we like our stew shaken or stirred, *James (the first)* asks? Everyone loves this joke – laughter ripples up and down the queue.

We'll have it shaken, please.

Moving on down the counter, here's Charles Darwin, the man in charge of the puddings. The *first Charles* we've met, he is today's King *Charles I*.

Now, be careful not to make any jokes with Charles,

especially not ones about the evolution of his puddings. He's been serving the same sweetened stew for as long as anyone can remember, and gets a bit touchy when anyone suggests intelligently designing a new one.

Uh-oh! Did you hear that? Trouble's brewing – the boy just behind us in the queue is demanding crumble for pudding. More than that, he wants olive crumble. Someone shut him up!

But it's too late.

'*Olive crumble?*' splutters Charles I.

'I demand it!' says the boy, *Oliver Cromwell*.

29

Things are about to get way out of hand – and now, out of nowhere and with a deafening roar, Cromwell leaps over the counter and slam-dunks a whole tray of stew over Charles's royal head!

Before you know it, pandemonium! We're in a full-blown food fight. Stew is flying in all directions, tables are being overturned and everyone is getting stuck in. It's almost impossible to see who is on which side, so we'll just plug away for king or country – or both . . . whatever.

After several minutes of joyous food fight, the battle subsides: everyone's run out of stew. But this isn't great news – Charles I, the pudding chef, has lost his head and, worse, Oliver Cromwell's been appointed head chef.

But what are they thinking? We have to run a marathon later! He'll try to feed us olive crumble as a main!

And the cheek! Cromwell is on the PA system telling us he's doing this to 'protect us', that we're now in a 'Protectorate'. What nonsense!

We loudly set to protesting the Protectorate, of course, and eventually we get our way: Stew is restored to its rightful position at the top, bottom and middle of the menu.

Hurrah for this restoration! We take a steaming plate of the good stuff and settle down outside with Charlie Chaplin, one of our best mates. He's just joined us for lunch. The *second Charles* we've met today, Charlie Chaplin represents *Charles II*. He's currently doing a very entertaining impression of some dancing legs with a couple of bread rolls stuck on a pair of forks.

And get a mouthful of this post-Restoration stew! It's much improved – with lots of fruit and veg in the swill, and no chocolate or chicken nuggets in sight. Who could the new chef be?

Hey, cool, the new chef's arrived to ask how we like his food and it's Jamie Oliver! How utterly, gloriously wonderful! We have half his books at home – but who would have guessed he'd be serving us at school? How kind of him to offer us a second helping.

Our *second James*, then, will be remembered as *James II*.

So our 'Stuarts' have been a palindrome: James, Charles and then Charles, James. And that eejit Oliver Cromwell wedged ingloriously in the middle.

What a feast – we've eaten well. And I'm glad we did: the first race begins in a few minutes. We were desperately in need of the energy.

Right, let's get changed. Follow me.

The entrance for the changing rooms is just through these orange doors leading off the dining courtyard. There we go – I'll hold the door for you.

So that's the House of Stuart we're done with, and this is the House of Orange. Whoa! I'd have brought my sunglasses if I'd known just how orange these changing rooms were going to be. This'll give me a migraine if I stay here too long.

Once your eyes have adjusted, though, look – you can see we've bumped into another young shepherdess called Mary, with another little lamb. This Mary differs from Bloody Mary, you'll notice, both in that she's not intent on eating or otherwise violating her lamb, and in that her 'lamb' is actually a goat. He's a billy goat.

Mary's teaching him to walk because he's lost his front left leg, and only has three remaining. Look how he lists to the left, unable to prevent himself from walking in circles, anti-clockwise. He's doing it now, despite Mary II's best efforts.

A tender scene. They ruled together, did *William III* and *Mary II*, our next monarchs.

Once kitted out, on our way out of the changing rooms we almost trip over a figure on the floor. It's Anne Robinson, pulling on her running spikes on the edge of the grass. Anne Robinson is *Queen Anne*, the last monarch of the House of Orange.

Queen Anne's got some banter up her sleeve, surprise surprise. She's telling us that we're the weakest link in our relay team.

We'll see about that, Anne.

All in all, then, in the House of Orange, we've met the three-legged William and his dear love Mary, and Queen Anne. And that's it.

Let's go over to the athletics track, where the relay is about to begin.

Team *Hanover* (famous across the district for their neat handovers) comprises four German boys called George. Each **George** has a different **form of transport** – a pogo stick, a bicycle, a trike and a four-wheeled steam engine car make up the team – and they're carefully arranged up the track, ready to go. This surely puts them at an advantage over us: we're just running.

And before we have a chance to sort out some devious strategy, the starter's pistol has gone and we're off!

32

George I gets a terrific start, hopping along like mad on his pogo stick in front of us. He duly hands over to the cyclist, *George II*. The cyclist races ahead to hand over to *George III*, the star of the show, who truly devours the next sixty yards on his recumbent trike – a three-wheeled bike, on which you lie back very close to the ground. As feared, the Hanoverians are running away with it.

But look – George III on the trike is losing the plot! He's just screeched to a sudden halt in the middle of the track,

well short of the handover point to *George IV*. The spectators are doing everything to urge him on, but he's refusing to budge.

George IV now has to reverse his steam engine backwards to grab the baton from the George on the trike. The time it takes him to back up allows us to sprint past, taking the lead, and, despite a tremendous effort from the steam-powered George IV, we're first over the line, breaking the ribbon. Hurrah!

Or rather – oh my God, this hurts!

We've just been skewered by the four sharp horns of a massive billy goat, one of the Hanoverian reserves, who has gone and head-butted us on the finishing line. We're now stuck on the four horns, suspended in the air as he trots around, snorting.

This *four-pronged* Hanoverian *billy* goat is obviously our fourth William, *William IV*. At last – goodness knows how

we do it – we manage to pull ourselves away just in time for the medal ceremony.

As victors over the Hanoverians, we're honoured to climb the podium and have a gold medal strung round our necks by none other than *Queen Victoria*, the last of the Hanoverian royals.

'Well done on your *victory*,' says Victoria.

Splendid. As she hangs the medals on us, we notice that her son (dressed in a very gothic outfit) is playing the national anthem on a tenor saxophone made of wood. How proud it makes you feel!

If you watch this Edward tooting his sax high in the air, you'll see that it makes the silhouette of the number seven against the sky.

The saxophonist is *Edward VII*, our next king. He is the only member of his band, which he's catchily called 'The House of Saxe-Coburg-Gotha'. He's considering changing the name. It sounds a bit German.

Meanwhile, sports day is far from over. Indeed, the longest and most prestigious event, the marathon, has yet to begin. It's a monster, this race! We have to run all the way to Buckingham Palace, a distance of twenty-six miles.

The starting line is between two wind turbines on the edge of the field. An extraordinary variety of competitors –humans, vehicles, animals – is already lining up between the two *wind* turbines, which mark the onset of the House of *Windsor*.

And the moment we take our position on the starting line, the starting gun fires. We're off again.

Hoooo – this is a bit quick. Not the gentle pace I was imagining. They'd better slow down soon. You know what? I hate cross-country. Surely you do as well. I can't be bothered to run twenty-six miles, and I bet you can't either. Let's just hop on the back of this tank, and leave all the physical agony to the other competitors.

Securely perched, we leave the school behind us and try to work out who this tank driver might be. Well, he must be *George V*: not just because he's got a mode of transport and we've already had four of those – each called George – but also because he has two gun-barrels on his tank, which split off in different directions forming a 'V'. For good measure, he keeps saying, 'Ready, aim, *five*.'

It feels like we've been bumping along for ages and, judging by the swelling crowds, we're nearing the finishing straight. Probably about time to hop off.

Go on, jump for it!

All we need to do now – watch! – is stretch our legs and motor in towards the finish with a modest but decisive lead.

In no time we're at the palace gates that mark the finishing line, striding along in first place.

And listen to the thunderous sound they make, these gates – they've clearly been turned into an organ for the

occasion. *Eight* massive wooden pipes extend far into the air, booming their celebratory tune. This organ is being played by the next king – no prizes for guessing that he is *Edward VIII*.

Forgive me for feeling that this must be just about the most suave marathon win the school has ever known. We've almost skipped under the organ into the palace courtyard without a bead of sweat on us. The crowd roars its appreciation; we politely celebrate. Excellent.

So we're now into Buckingham Palace's forecourt – on which a spanking spitfire gleams in the sunlight: what a beauty. It has six wings – a clever aerodynamic device, no doubt – and it represents *George VI*. Go on, then – it also has a big '6' on the side.

My goodness – this is our prize for winning! A George VI Spitfire! Rather generous, but we'll take it!

We must be ever so close to the end of the day. Looking upwards, indeed we are! Take a look at this! There she is! It's the queen, the real queen! Our very own *Queen Elizabeth II*! She's waving at us! How cool is this? She's on her balcony waving straight at us!

The perfect end to the perfect day – she's coming down to kiss us!

At this, of course, we faint.

On regaining consciousness, the queen, the Spitfire and the crowd have all disappeared. We have only our memories to cherish. But what memories!

Let's quickly run over them a last time to make sure that they'll never be forgotten.

We were woken at 7.57 a.m. by the warlord Offa dumping loads of offal on us. We hastened to the bathroom where a burst egg, King Egbert, was in the bath. The sink was taken too – by a wolf in a bottle, Aethelwulf, cleaning himself with three of his sons. First, Aethelbald the roll-on deodorant; next, Aethelbert the bird, whose whirring beak clipped his moustache; and the last of the three aethels on the shelf was the red lipstick bottle, Aethelred.

Breakfast beckoned. On the landing, Alfred was making an all-fried fry-up, but we didn't feel like it so we made off down the stairs. At the top, we found a wooden head being swept down some elderflower rapids – that was Edward the Elder. At the bottom, we collided into a couple of bottles of fake tan, Aethelstan.

Entering the kitchen, we almost tripped over Edmund the Magnificent's head-mound on the floor.

But we wanted some cornflakes so we forged on. Opening the fridge, Edred's ketchup had obscured the milk and when a boy in a soggy head-wig (King Eadwig or Edwy) peered out of the dishwasher, we gave up on cornflakes altogether. We thought the oven offered hope, but instead it contained a very relaxed head lighting his cigar off the grill – that was Edgar the Peaceable.

A little annoyed by this point, we went to the sink to get ourselves a glass of water. There we met the muttering wooden head, King Edward, whom we martyred.

Glass of water in hand, we took the Aethelred Ribena from the kitchen table and added a taste of it to our water. Delicious. That bottle was our last Wessex kitchen king.

In search of Danish pastries, we set off for the sitting room – the House of Denmark – where Sven with his forked beard was stuck on the sofa (Sweyn Forkbeard) with a second mound of heads, Edmund II, piled up at his feet.

Canute the Great was a huge canoe balanced on the TV, but we peered past his legs to see an episode of *Neighbours* where hairy-footed Harold Harefoot was being run over by Harthacanute, one half of a canoe.

Harthacanute was the last of the Kings of Denmark, and we found our last two Wessex kings in the drive: Edward the Confessor confessing to crushing our car, and a second Harold at the garden gate.

To the bus stop, then, where we found Billy one and two: the Conqueror whacking his conker against the outside of the shelter, and the roofless Rufus sleeping inside.

The school bus pulled in and a fluffy chick, Henry I, tried to buy a ticket from King Stephen Fry, the bus driver. Suddenly Empress Matilda crashed in with her anger-van.

In the anger-van of the House of Angevin, we were driven by Henry II (the two-headed hen) while Richard I (Branson) hung out with his younger brother, John (Travolta), on the roof.

Henry III, the peacock with three 'eyes' in his tail, met us at the Plantagenet school gates, and in the bike sheds we had Eds I, II and III making music on a bass-drum, some bongos and a triad of didgeridoos. Richard and Judy, Richard II, seemed to like what they saw from their nearby sofa.

Off went the school bus and suddenly there we were at

the lanky-red-rose classroom register where Henry IV, the four-ton turkey, was signing in the five peregrine falcons of Henry V and the six penguins of Henry VI. The lanky red roses of course signified that this was the House of Lancaster.

Among the stalks of the white roses of the York staircase on the way to science, we met Eddie IV on bass guitar, accompanied (silently) by the air-guitar-strumming, cricket-bat-wielding Eddie V. Three-legged Ricky Gervaise, bad King Richard III, looked down from the top of the stairs as he practised for the three-legged race.

In our two-door science lab, where we met six Tudors in all, we first encountered an eagle, Henry VII, who was teaching (mainly to the class pet, Henry VIII – the eight-foot ostrich). At the back, Edward VI played us a few little tunes to dance along to.

In the second part of science we did the experiments, with Lady Jane Grey inventing Lady Grey tea, and Bloody Mary inventing a Bloodier Mary. On the back bench Cate Blanchett was putting lizards to bed – that was the looker, Elizabeth I.

Fond memories of a stewed Stuart lunch next! James I (played by Sean Connery) giving us our stew; Charles I (Darwin) trying to give us even more; and then that storming internal food fight caused by Oliver Cromwell's obnoxious demands.

After the Restoration (of order) we lunched with our chum Charlie Chaplin, Charles II, before Jamie Oliver, James II, came to check out how it had all gone.

We'd no sooner shaken his hand than we were rushing to get changed, for sports day was about to start. In the House of Orange, the changing rooms, we met Mary II and William III, a shepherdess training her three-legged billy goat to walk; then, on the lip of the sports field, Queen Anne (Robinson).

Out on the sports fields we raced the Hanoverians,.

Georges I to IV, out on the track, and were caught in the four horns of their billy-goat associate, William IV, at the finish line.

Victoria soon gave us a medal, though, to the tune of Edward VII's national anthem on the sax.

Sports day finished with a marathon: we rode with George V on his tank all the way to the palace gates, where Edward VIII, the last of our Edwards, boomed his congratulations on a wooden organ. Having passed through the organ into the forecourt we were awarded George VI in his Spitfire as a prize, and were finally completely overwhelmed, when Queen Elizabeth II herself skipped down the steps to give us a kiss. Marvellous.

ROUND TWO: SPOTTING THE DETAIL

Morale is the muesli of memory, so to speak – the source of slow-release energy that keeps your remembering fresh and energetic, capable of pushing on forward. For this reason, before you take on this second geeky section (where we'll be filling in some of the historical detail to go with our kings and queens), you need to make sure you're feeling pretty good about what you've learnt already.

The best way to feel good is to astonish someone, and, where possible, to win some money from them as you do so. Before you pile into this section, therefore, I recommend accosting a relative, a co-worker or perhaps a pedestrian and betting a fiver on your ability to recite the chronology of kings and queens – backwards, if necessary.

Having collected the money, retire to a warm, dry place and get stuck into this, our second pass over the same monarchs as before. The aim of the game is to learn a few choice facts and something of the character of all the monarchs. The rules are the same – if you imagine what happens vividly, you won't forget it in a hurry.

1

So, off we go, then. We'll begin again in our royal bed, with **King Offa** of Mercia dumping his bucket of offal on our faces. What's to add? Well, look here how a mud wall, running through the bedroom, divides it in two and how, up against this mud dyke, a poor *whale*'s been spectacularly beached.

This is a smaller version of the historical Offa's Dyke, which to this day runs along most of the border between Mercia and *Wales*.

2

Continuing on into the House of Wessex and the bathroom, look how the tiles round **Egbert**'s bath are actually squares of corn bread that have been neatly stuck together, covering the wall. This bathroom's clearly been *bread-walled* – a neat reminder of Egbert's self-proclaimed title: *bretwalda*, which means 'ruler of Britain' in Anglo-Saxon.

And fancy this – one of those bread tiles is falling down on a *hinge* made from *stone*, a secret door! Out of this door a Viking pops, followed soon after by his warlike pals. But they've timed their invasion poorly – the bursting egg covers them in yolk before they've taken even three steps. Note how the exact time of the egg burst is 8.38 a.m.

What does this all mean? Well, Vikings being destroyed at 8.38 a.m. in the *cornwall* when the *hinge-o'-stone's down* reminds us of how Egbert's great military victory against the Vikings was at Hingston Down in Cornwall in the year 838.

3

Over to the sink, where the shampoo in **Aethelwulf**'s bottle is Øs-burga brand, shampoo to kings, no less. It's been made from liquefied ostrich burgers, very fragrant. Please don't ask what they put in ninth-century conditioners. Osburga is also the name of Aethelwulf's first wife, by the way, and mother of the next four kings.

4, 5+6

The three Aethels in their bottles on the shelf (**Aethelbald**, **Athelbert** and **Aethelred**) have been numbered in order – Baldy is 4, Bertie is 5 and Red is 6. They are our fourth, fifth and sixth kings, and they reigned for four, five and six years respectively. All very neat.

If you look more closely at the mirror above the sink, you'll notice it doubles as a cupboard door. Opening it up, a massive pile of flesh slobbers out (about 865 pounds of it) and crushes, or perhaps engorges is the word, our poor Aethelbert. This flesh-pile is Ivor the Boneless, leader of the AD 865 Viking invasion in which Aethelbert was killed.

At this point Mrs *Merton* appears at the sink. A cross-dresser, she needs some lipstick. She grabs Aethelred and slathers on so much of him that soon nothing remains of the poor king.

And indeed overworked Aethelred died fighting against the invading Danes in AD 871 – at the Battle of *Merton*.

7

If kings four, five and six lasted four, five and six years, you would think that **Alfred**, our seventh, would last seven, wouldn't you? But not a chance! He's four times greater than that, and will last for twenty-eight years. Let's take a closer look at him.

He is still on the landing, of course, cooking breakfast. He's frying up a cake on a roaring fire whose golden flames can mean only one thing: it's being fed with gold. Alfred found that bribing the Vikings with gold was the best way to get them to clear off. But something must be on his mind – it's been so long since he turned his cake that it's fizzing, spluttering and beginning to let off black smoke. He must be making a name for himself as the 'king who burnt the cakes'.

You may be thinking that the hefty tome of philosophy at Alfred's side is a bit showy, but, on the contrary, Alfred is quietly making a translation (available at all good bookshops priced £8.99). He spent his old age producing such works, and died as 'the wisest of kings' in AD 899.

8

The thought of cornflakes ushers us onwards to the top of the stairs.

As we rocket down the elderflower rapids, clinging to the wooden head, a fishhook catches our shirt. Who could be *angling* on the stairs at this time of the morning?

It's the last thing you'd expect! A *whale* is fishing out of the back of his *Mercedes*, which the silly mammal's parked on a window sill above the stream. Fortunately, Edward and our combined momentum are too much for the angling whale, and we pull him, Merc and all, into the water behind us.

Just so were *Mercia*, *East Anglia* and parts of *Wales* pulled by **Edward the Elder** into his kingdom.

9

The 920s was the first point in England's history where there was any unity of fashion: everyone in England was wearing this fake tan. The nation went orange. But this was inevitable, I suppose, because **Aethelstan** was the first king of all of current-day England.

10

Onwards to the kitchen where it's good to see that **Edmund the Magnificent** is wearing WWII army gear on his head-mound. He reigned from 939 to 946, so he was exactly a thousand years ahead of his time. And look – there's a thief trying to nick one of the female heads from his mound. '*Lay off her!*' Edmund shouts. But the thief *Leofa* takes her anyway, causing the whole mound to collapse – burying both himself and the king. Edmund and this thief, Leofa, killed each other in a fight at Pucklechurch.

11

There's more violence afoot by the fridge: Eric Clapton is creeping up on the open door, intending to hack **Edred** to death with his guitar-cum-axe. At the last moment, though, Edred knocks the axe from Eric's hand with a well-aimed spurt of ketchup (or is it blood?) and Eric, whose white shirt is stained more than he can bear, collapses in a lifeless heap, his *axe* covered in *blood*. This is none other than Eric Bloodaxe, whom Edred had killed at the battle of Stainmore in 954.

12

Reopening the dishwasher, we find **Eadwig** has been joined in his cloud of steam by a pretty young girl; they're having a party. It's ravetastic. But he knows he should really be at his coronation banquet.

'If I'm not back soon, they'll never forgive me,' he explains to his love interest.

'*I'll forgive you*,' says Aelfgifu, pushing him playfully against the cutlery holder. Rather disappointingly for those of us who feel this is leading somewhere, a bishop blunders in, ruining the moment.

'I don't understand,' splutters the bishop. 'I just dun'stan' why you're here and not eating with the nobles.'

This is Bishop Dunstan, by the way, this man who doesn't understand and disapproves of King **Edwy**. The cheeky Edwy responds to the interruption by weeing in the general direction of the bishop, offending Dunstan so deeply that he runs off.

13

Dunstan wouldn't return to England after this till the reign of **Edgar.**

On the subject of whom – here Edgar is again, thoughtfully carving up a cake of Great Britain into amusing new shapes as he smokes away in the oven.

This reminds us how the historical Edgar realigned the county boundaries, and baked them in so thoroughly that they lasted for 1,000 years until 1974.

14

In the frothing sink is **Edward the Martyr** – imagine this, he's being drowned by an elf in the froth! This imaginary elf is Elfthryth, Aethelred's mother.

15

Elfthryth had Edward murdered so that her own son, **Aethelred**, could become king. Although a very large bottle – 38 litres – her son Aethelred is unfortunately leaking his red liquid everywhere. There won't be much left if he carries on like this.

And during his disastrous thirty-eight years on the throne Aethelred did indeed disperse the entirety of what had been a stable and prosperous kingdom – into the hands of the Vikings.

Aethelred's wife, Baby Spice as it happens, is doing her best to mop up after him. To do so, she's standing on a footstool mopping up with a yellow cloth.

Now it's good we get to meet Emma (of Normandy) because she was wife to two kings, mother to two and stepmother to two. For those readers who secretly harbour the intention to marry one of our eligible young royals, Emma stands as a shining example of what can be achieved with hard work, focus and, they say, almost insane levels of beauty.

From now on we'll have the following code: if you see Emma herself, that means the king she is with is her husband. Where there's a footstool to *step on*, well, that's her stepson, and where there's conspicuous *sun*shine, that's her *son* shining.

16

Onwards to the House of Denmark!

Sweyn's still stuck on the sofa, making an emergency call on his mobile phone. It's a Bluetooth-enabled phone, made by Ericsson of course: **Sweyn Forkbeard** was the son of the Danish warrior-king Bluetooth.

17

Edmund II Ironside, meanwhile, has the misfortune of needing the toilet. For an assassin is hidden in the latrine, and takes the opportunity to launch his sword up the king's backside. Spillage resulted. The remarkable thing is that King Edmund's death, skewered like this while on the toilet, isn't even the most horrible in English history. For that, you'll have to wait.

18

Pass your attention now to our telly-top canoe, where Emma Bunton has joined **Canute** (Emma of Normandy married him, after all). Fluttering in the breeze on the back of the canoe are the flags of Norway, Sweden, Denmark and England. He's earned such varied nationality, to be sure: Canute was king of all these countries, and ruled more lands besides.

19

The situation on *Neighbours*, meanwhile, is that **Harold**'s taken the crown because Harthacanute is stuck fighting in Denmark on the other side of the river.

Let's rejoin the action. Harold's waiting nervously on his footstool in the river (he's Emma's stepson, you see) as half a canoe struggles across from the battlefields of Scandinavia to claim his crown – by force. The sun shines brightly on Harthacanute's yellow canoe; he's Emma's son.

20

Unfortunately for the viewing public, just at the moment where **Harthacanute** arrives, when we can reasonably expect a bit of juicy violence, Harold has (or fakes – how's one to know?) an epileptic fit and topples dead into the water – *splosh!* – depriving us of the fight scene we deserve. There wasn't even contact between the two of them. Lame.

21

Outside, **Edward the Confessor** seems to fall from the sky like a fireball, such is the glare that shines off his polished face from the bright morning sun (he's another of Emma's sons). And, as you can see from this car wreck, he was responsible during his reign for a massive breakdown (in royal power, style and prestige).

22

By the gate, it's quite fun watching **Harold** vainly trying to deal with the people who keep crashing his garden. First up, a couple of kids in Chelsea football kit. Harold agrees to take them on in a game of football; he's really got no choice. He wins comfortably. Hurrah! This is the Battle of Stamford Bridge of 1066.

But poor Harold has such terrible luck – he's still puffed out when the big billy goat shows up, demanding to be let in. Harold tries to stop him, but the goat whacks him in the eye with the conker, and Harold staggers back, collapsing into a convenient *haystack*. This is the Battle of *Hastings*, where Harold and his army (exhausted after Stamford Bridge) were defeated, alas, by William the Conqueror.

23

Over by that normal bus stop, the House of Normandy, where **William the Conqueror** is bashing the bus stop, there's an advert for a new bestseller, with the catchy caption 'There's no escaping the Doomsday Book'. Accurate advertising: it being true that everyone had to report exactly what they owned for that vast national database.

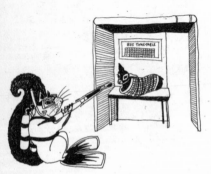

24

And, inside the shelter, our vulnerable, roofless **William II Rufus** is being stalked by a squirrel with snorkel, flippers and harpoon. It is a hunting aquatic squirrel – this water squirrel is Walter Tirel. But no! Poor William Rufus! See now as Tirel the squirrel shoots him in the head with his harpoon! Hear that gruesome crunching sound!

William Rufus was murdered by Walter Tirel, a friend of Henry I, in a 'hunting accident' in the New Forest.

25

Just then, the school bus pulls up and our fluffy white chick tries to clamber on board. But either that rucksack full of treasure is just too heavy for him, or he's been eating too much. Oh dear – as he falls, a tumble of eel-like fish spills from his beak. Greedy **Henry I** is the only king to die from an addiction to lampreys, of which 'he ate a surfeit'.

The treasure, meanwhile, reminds us that this king was also responsible for important developments in the treasury.

26

The bus driver, **Stephen** Fry, is Henry's cousin. 'Are you OK, coz?' he asks the overfed chick before him, but gets no response.

At exactly this moment, Matilda's anger-van (which has a big *anarchy* symbol on the side) rams the side of the bus. The ensuing argument with Matilda quickly spreads: all down Norman Street people are taking up their doormats to whack each other on the head.

27

This civil war, splendidly known as 'The Anarchy' (1135–54), of course finally lands Matilda's son **Henry II** in the driving seat (of the anger-van) as the first king of the House of Angevin.

Henry II immediately puts the pedal to the metal while his beautiful wife, Eleanor of Aquitaine, *leans* across him to light his cigarette. She doesn't smoke herself – she's *quit*, and she's looking leaner for it, is old E*lean*or of A*quit*aine.

The back of the school bus is usually the coolest place to sit but not on this one – twelve angry men are arranged round a table debating someone's guilt: it's a jury, a legal implement Henry II introduced to England in 1166.

28+29

Richard is meanwhile sitting directly above the driver on the roof, now filling in his year planner. Looking at his busy schedule, he notes that he'll mainly be raiding Jerusalem this year, like the last.

In his ten years on the throne, **Richard the Lionheart** spent just ten months in England whilst most of his time was spent crusading in the Middle East.

John Travolta, meanwhile, at the back of the roof, is being bullied by some other boys. They are making him sign a piece of paper that says he's a loser good-for-nothing king, the kind of king bound by the rule of law. He's signing away his basic rights as king in the Magna Carta of 1215.

But he's soon laughing at them, saying he was crossing his fingers behind his back all along. They're furious, of course, which will no doubt remind you of the troubles that followed John's rejection of the very power-limiting document he'd himself signed.

30

Enough of this, the van has come to a halt at the three-level pagoda that represents the school gates.

We may as well check out what goes on inside. On the first floor we find a room covered in the plans for various English cathedrals – a kind of architect's cubby-hole.

Up on the second level, we disturb the entrance exams for Oxford University and tiptoe out, mumbling our apologies.

Up at the top, noisy adults sit on green benches jeering at each other – we're in an early parliament.

These three levels reflect the grand achievements of **Henry III**'s kingship: the building of vast cathedrals, the foundation of Oxford University and the beginnings of the Houses of Parliament.

Clambering down the fifty-six steps (one for each year in Henry III's reign), we slip through the school gates and into the Plantagenet playground.

31-3

The bike-shed concert is still going strong. The three Eds are really letting fly, though each seems to be playing his own tune.

Edward I is hammering hard on his tartan drum, trying to bring down the walls of Jericho by the sounds of things. The 'Hammer of the Scots' was a great wall-builder in his own right, constructing hundreds of castles during his reign.

Edward II has been joined at the bongos by a boy whose nose has been pierced by a *carved stone*, a guy called *Pierş Gaverstone*. The two of them look like they're in love.

This surely won't please Eddie II's girlfriend, Isabella, who's known in school as the 'she-wolf' for her vicious temper.

Is that *a bell* I hear? It is! See how Isabella the she-wolf pads in now with a bell tinkling on her neck and a red-hot poker between her jaws. With breathtaking brutality she thrusts the red-hot poker, I'm afraid, into Ed II's bottom. It is rumoured that Edward II's wife, Isabella, ordered his brutal murder in this fashion – I think this outdoes Edmund II's demise for gruesome splendour, no?

Edward III's three didgeridoos point out towards Richard and Judy on their sofa.

Cress sandwiches tumble from the first instrument while the middle one, painted black, is rattling alarmingly with the sound of human bones. The third didgeridoo, meanwhile, has been placed in a potty to collect all the saliva dribbling from it. Nice.

The black one with its rattling bones reminds us of the Black Death of 1348. The cress and the potty remind us of Ed's two great victories at Crécy (1346) and Poitiers (1356) – against the French.

The combined sound of these didgeridoos will reverberate for the next century as these battles set in motion the Hundred Years' War for the French throne. Right up until the middle of the penguins' reign, we'll be able to hear this lugubrious droning sound.

34

Richard and Judy don't have the necessary peace and quiet to enjoy the music, sadly, for some revolting peasants are pelting them with rotten fruit and veg. King **Richard II** tells them to calm down, quite effectively actually, for they troop off home, allowing Richard to concentrate on the important business of inventing the handkerchief.

35

Henry IV, the four-ton turkey who does the register, looks like he's been waiting for class to settle down forever. But he's actually been scheming himself. I don't know if you saw this, but he recently murdered Rich and Judy by suffocating them beneath a tea towel. He still has the murder implement to hand (it's got the London tube map printed on it).

This tea towel of London stands for the Tower of London, that dungeon of horrors. Since the Tower of London features quite a lot in English history, we'll be seeing this tea towel again. So make a note: tea towel means tower.

So Henry IV deposed Richard II, and threw him in the Tower of London – where he was later murdered, or possibly just starved to death, in the year 1400. Back in the classroom, Henry IV's register is continually interrupted by crowds of rebellious kids leaning in the window to heckle him. These girls and boys still believe that Richard and Judy are alive, and that Henry shouldn't be king. (Rich and Judy are dead, of course; it's just that their pre-recorded programme continues to air each morning.)

Just so did Henry IV spend much of his time dealing with insurrections and rebellions, with many of his citizens still believing that Richard II remained alive. This hullabaloo is making it impossible to maintain discipline in the classroom, and isn't helped by the sound of that Hundred Years' War didgeridoo still droning away in the bike shed.

36

Henry V, our V-formation of peregrine falcons, now adds to the mayhem by reliving yesterday's match against the French at the Battle of Agincourt.

Out come their longbows as they pepper the wall with arrows, exchanging high fives as they reminisce over their acts of derring-do. 'There were thousands of them, but we sure as heck nailed the lot of them.'

Unfortunately, after only a few minutes of this, all the falcons die suddenly of dysentery.

How unfortunate that the king of *de century*, the legendary king who won us the Battle of Agincourt, should die of *dysentery*.

37

Our huddle of **Henry VI**s at the back look remarkably like they're dressed in the Eton school uniform, don't they? But this should come as no surprise, because Henry VI founded Eton College (and King's College, Cambridge, with it) during his reign.

But let's follow the penguins now, as they march in single file for double science. As we go along, the sound of the didgeridoo and the Hundred Years' War fades away (after 116 years).

38

At the stairs of York, the sound of a bass guitar immediately flumps into our ears; bass guitarist **Edward IV** is blocking our way. He's made an obstacle of himself, erecting a stage from thousands of books – they're suddenly two a penny since England's first printing press got into operation during his reign.

Our penguin guide, a great believer in flower power, starts launching *red* roses aggressively at the bassist. Edward IV returns fire with some white ones. Yes, people, we are in the War of the Roses. When Edward loses patience with the ineffective rose weapon, he lobs a giant tea towel over the heads of our penguin huddle.

That's right: Edward IV resorted to the tea-towel treatment when reclaiming his throne, throwing his adversary Henry VI to a nasty death in the tower.

39

Just behind this chaotic scene, **Edward V** is still air-guitaring away. He's actually on the way to recruiting a whole (pretend) band, if you look – what with his little brother, Little Richard, miming along beside.

40

But three-legged **Richard III**, hunchbacked Ricky Gervaise, is creeping down from the stairs towards Edward V and his brother – and is that another tea towel in his hands? Indeed it is.

Ricky III has swooped up Edward V and his brother Richard in the towel, smuggling them to their death in the tower. These were then the so-called *Princes in the Tower*, rumours of whose disastrous fate still echo to this day.

41

Phew! We're off the staircase and into double science. Inscribed above the two doors of the House of Tudor, the date reads 1485.

At the front of the class, **Henry VII** is making good use of the overhead projector to show us his wedding snaps.

He's obviously chuffed with his new lizard bride, whose beautiful dress is made entirely from white rose petals. This lizard of York is Elizabeth of York, and her white petals mix beautifully with his Lancastrian red to make the red-and-white Tudor rose.

One very entertaining picture is of the married couple cutting their cake, which is a Simnel cake. At the moment they jointly push down, you can see Lambert Simnel, pretender to the throne, bursting out of the middle, playing air-guitar and shouting, 'I'm King Edward V.' Very funny.

Henry VII quite stylishly ordered Simnel to work in the royal kitchens after he tried to steal the crown by pretending to be Edward V. It was in these kitchens that he's rumoured to have invented the Simnel cake.

The lesson gets underway.

42

In the front row, **Henry VIII**, our eight-foot ostrich, is not alone: six of his girlfriends join him there, three to either side. But you know that Henry VIII had six wives.

More interestingly, look at this – Henry has rebelliously taken a jar of acid and he's *dissolving* wads of *money* in the fizzing liquid. This is some kind of protest, and by his *dissolution* of the *monasteries*, Henry VIII created the Protestant Church of England.

Since the ensuing history of the royal household is dominated by infighting within the Christian church, we need to be able to recognize our Protestants from our Catholics: where we have someone *protesting* in some way, they are a *Protestant*. *Catholics* will be spotted by a *cat licking* at them.

43

At the back, then, Ed VI, a ten-year-old, is tooting away on his recorder, playing protest songs. Think about it . . . Next to him you can see how his mate Thomas the Tank Engine is cramming copies of the newly released Book of Common Prayer into his funnel.

During the young **Edward VI**'s brief reign, *Thomas Cramner* introduced this important book.

44

In the lab, Lady Jane Grey is also mounting a small protest – she's another protestant. She is such a goodie two-shoes, though, that her idea of a protest is to make her own variety of tea when she should be making the plain stuff.

In any case, she only has time to brew it for a lame nine seconds, because Mary is wandering over with a tea towel, disgusted at this protest(ant). We know what the tea towel means for poor Jane, don't we? So that was the end of **Lady Jane Grey** – her death in The Tower came after only nine days on the throne.

45

Look at this! Mary, having dealt with Jane Grey, is setting out on a rampage about the classroom with her Bunsen burner, burning anyone she suspects of protesting. She's left her cocktail in the capable paws of a cat that licks up the potent liquid with great aplomb.

Catholic **Queen Mary**'s 'Marian Persecutions' resulted in her burning at least 300 Protestants at the stake.

46

But Mary's death brings her half-sister, **Elizabeth I**, to the throne, a woman whose quiet protest has gone unnoticed during the Marian massacre. It takes an unusual form: she's training her lizards to perform a subversive forty-five-minute-long play, written by Shakespeare, whose scenes include a battle involving the Spanish Armada, the discovery of the New World and a warty fellow juggling potatoes while cycling on a Raleigh bike smoking a cigarette.

With Shakespearian drama, the defeat of the Spanish, the conquest of the New World and Sir Walter Raleigh's (related) introduction of potatoes and tobacco, the Elizabethan era is still warmly remembered today as a happening forty-five years.

47

Over in the dining hall Sean Connery, our **James I**, is Scottish, of course – and he proudly presides over the Stuarts' stew. It is quite a collection of characters he's serving – Guy Fawkes and Pocahontas are waiting in line. There's even a rasher of bacon in a French baguette, Sir Francis Bacon, queuing up.

48

Along the counter, Charles Darwin's part of the kitchen looks fantastic with all the expensive portraits he's put up. **Charles I** was a great patron of the visual arts, and single-minded in his vision of the king's right to rule as he pleased.

So when Oliver Cromwell starts demanding olive crumble, he refuses to listen to the boy. His decapitation during the food fight that results is noteworthy for its dignity.

We shouldn't, meanwhile, dwell on the ugly story of Oliver Cromwell, who caused all this, for he was never king. From his selfish crumble demands we know already, I think, that he was a vicious and self-obsessed man.

49

Outside, while eating our food, **Charles II** drops from the branches of an oak tree to say a merry 'hi'. He's been hiding in this oak ever since the Battle of Worcester (sauce) during the latter stages of the food fight we just witnessed. This is what the pub name 'Royal Oak' refers to, incidentally.

He soon invites an alarmingly diverse collection of girlfriends down. Lunch in the company of the 'merry monarch' himself, Charles II, and his lovely ladies is quite enjoyable; the only thing to mar the meal is the neighbouring table, where diners are falling terribly ill, with horrible screams, before spontaneously combusting.

These experiences may help us recall how Charles II, aside from collecting mistresses, had to deal with such events as the Plague and the Great Fire (of London, not Wem) that took place in 1666.

50

With Jamie Oliver's arrival, we are initially delighted. But our joy turns to disgust when we see that he's letting his hand be licked by a mangy little cat.

We all agree that **James II**'s partiality to being licked by a cat, his Catholicism, is a major health-and-safety issue. So, we vote with our feet and tool onwards to the house of Orange.

James II was the first king removed by vote of parliament – who, in the so-called Glorious Revolution, invited his daughter, Mary (a nice, reliable hater of cats) to assume the throne instead – with the help of her Dutch husband. This all happened in 1688.

51

So, **William and Mary** (unusual joint
sovereigns) are still running round and
round in circles in their orange changing
room when a toucan asks for their
autographs. But while busy trying to *sign*
its colourful *bill* (a great big thing, the
perfect size for *writing* on) William trips on
a rogue molehill and falls to his death.

William and Mary *signed the Bill of
Rights*, limiting the monarch's power yet
further, and this was a great inspiration
for the American Declaration of Independence. William died of pneumonia after a
fall when his horse tripped on a molehill, and the mole, 'the little fellow in the velvet
waistcoat', was toasted by ribald Jacobites.

52

Next to Anne Robinson on the side of the
changing rooms, there are, quite alarmingly,
seventeen miniature tombstones scattered
about the place. The only one of **Queen
Anne**'s seventeen children to survive infancy
died at the age of eleven, which just goes to
show the state of medicine at the time.

But Anne is putting a brave face on
things – she's waving a Union Jack above her
head and she's got not one but two party hats
on. It was during Anne's reign in 1707 that the act of
Union occurred where Scotland officially joined England,
the two becoming Britain, and two-party politics also got going.

53

Out on the track, **George I**, on his pogo stick, is a short,
fat, unhealthy, poor-tempered old man – lacking in
any kind of charm. He nonetheless totters ahead
surprisingly fast on his pogo stick. (Impressive for a
fifty-four-year-old, the oldest age for a king to start his
reign so far.)

Instead of a baton, he's carrying a protest banner
(reading 'no cats on sports day!'), so all the English cheer him along
enthusiastically. He scowls – not only does he not understand what
they're saying (he speaks no English) but he has little regard for the people
over whom he reigns, who selected him for his staunch Protestantism.

He hands the banner-baton over in unorthodox fashion – by whacking
it over his son's head, their relationship being famously fractious.

54

George II, in full military uniform, races forward with his wife Caroline behind him on their tandem. He needs her help – he is being raced on the outside by a young Prince Charles on the dog Bonnie. It's Bonnie Prince Charlie, the young pretender to the throne. George II outstrips him, though

– which is the least you'd expect of the last English king to have fought in battle, and presently he hands over to his own son, continuing the family tradition by beating him over the head.

55

George III seems a pleasanter sort, but events off the track dominate his sixty-yard leg of the race. Most notably, some angry American athletes try to set up a breakaway sports event over on the other side of the track. At this, the loss of the American colonies, George III goes quite mad with rage, and stops in his tracks, unable to continue.

All the same, he does last sixty years on the throne, the longest so far.

56

George IV has to reverse his steam engine and take over the baton, even though it's not yet officially his go. This leg of the race is the so-called Regency – where George carries the baton for his father, who's too mad to do so himself.

George IV is enormously fat, by the way, hence the need for a steam engine. As he goes along, the steam from his funnel briefly forms the shape of a loo in the air – marking victory in the Battle of Waterloo in 1815.

When George III is finally removed from the track and it's officially our steam-engine driver's go, his lady-friend comes on to the track to celebrate but he pushes her away – just as the real George IV had his wife banned from his own coronation. Ouch.

57

As we cross the finish line ahead of G4 and clatter into our four-pronged goat, we knock a naval cap from its head. **William IV** was known as the Sailor King, having served in the Royal Navy.

It's a bit unclear how we'll ever escape from his horrible horns – they've pretty much got us trapped – but at the last moment they re-form, and we drop off and are free again to do as we please. This fortunate Reform Act (of 1832) gave normal people like us the freedom to vote (except for women – they had to wait. And under eighteens – they're still waiting).

58

Queen Victoria's winner's podium is made entirely of glass. It is a miniature model of the Crystal Palace, the iconic building of Victoria's reign. On the podium with us are an Indian girl and a Canadian man, this being the peak of the British Empire.

Victoria is so short (five feet tall) that she requires her beloved husband Albert to lift her up to deliver the medals. Hurrah! The only downside is the length of the ceremony, sixty-three minutes: a minute for each year of Victoria's record-breaking reign.

59

Edward VII, who's playing the national anthem in the French style, is enjoying the prospect of the approaching marathon. He actually owns several of the horses who'll be racing alongside us. Hmm ... worrying ... he's a terribly successful horse-owner.

He looks very chirpy and mightily relieved to be playing his sax at last, and who can blame him? He spent longer than our own Prince Charles waiting for his mother to pass on the spoon so he could have a go as king – much of which time was in France. There, he established the Entente Cordiale that is still around today.

60

As we hop on to the back of George's double-barrelled V-tank, we're not actually lost for things to do during the twenty-six-year marathon reign. For a start, there's WWI to cheer along, and then there's George V's incredible stamp collection to be enjoyed.

George V led Britain through WWI right into the thirties, though he avoided the public spotlight most of the time, preferring time with his stamps.

61

At the organ-gates, **Edward VIII** seems to be *walloping* out the theme tune to *The Simpsons* on his organ. He gets about six bars in and then gives up. This may remind us of how he abdicated the throne after only six months so that he could run off with an American lady named *Wallis Simpson*.

62

Passing the organ into the courtyard, we notice that the rather smart Spitfire, this means of transport that will take us through WWII, is actually being driven by the Queen Mother, who was George VI's wife. She's trying to start the plane now – but the engine is misfiring, stuttering terribly.

George VI had an awkward stutter, but worked hard at overcoming it after unexpectedly acceding to the throne, and was much admired, not least for his supreme wife.

63

And **Queen Elizabeth II** – waving at us from the balcony – well, there's no need to elaborate on her evident perfection, is there?

KINGS AND QUEENS

Offa	Edward III
Egbert	Richard II
Aethelwulf	Henry IV
Aethelbald	Henry V
Aethelbert	Henry VI
Aethelred	Edward IV
Alfred the Great	Edward V
Edward the Elder	Richard III
Aethelstan	Henry VII
Edmund the Magnificent	Henry VIII
Edred	Edward VI
Eadwig/ Edwy	Lady Jane Grey
Edgar the Peaceable	Mary I
Edward the Martyr	Elizabeth I
Aethelred the Unready	James I
Sweyn Forkbeard	Charles I
Edmund Ironside	Charles II
Canute the Great	James II
Harold Harefoot	William and Mary
Harthacanute	Anne
Edward the Confessor	George I
Harold II	George II
William the Conqueror	George III
William 'Rufus' II	George IV
Henry I	William IV
Stephen	Victoria
Henry II	Edward VII
Richard the Lionheart	George V
John	Edward VIII
Henry III	George VI
Edward I	Elizabeth II
Edward II	

THE PRESIDENTS OF THE USA

N ow this is much more fun than a history lesson:
our chauffeur-driven limo, with police motorbike
outriders, is giving the traffic the
Red Sea treatment, and look at
this – we're just flying along to the
airport. Could this be what they
call the American Dream.

Can you hear the 'Star-spangled
Banner' now pumping out of our
super-charged sound system,
putting us in the mood for our
trip to the USA?

Hello: our driver's winding the glass screen down to ask
us if we'd like him to juice up the volume and learn all the
US presidents on our way to the plane.

That's a 'yes, please', chauffeur.

Did you get a look at him, by the way? You didn't? Well,
let me just knock on the glass and give you another chance
to inspect.

Oops – soap suds are coming in over the lowering pane
– I forgot to mention that our chauffeur's washing himself.
But don't feel scared that he's a dead-ringer for the shark
Jaws, for he's a friendly Jaws – called George. Sure, at first it
gives you a chill to look at rows upon rows of perfect white

teeth – but that's American dentistry for you.

A *Jaws* called *George* who *washes himself tons*? He's *George Washington*, the first president of the US of A.

On the subject of founding fathers, get an eyeful of the specimen opposite us over the drinks cabinet here in the back, this big apple on the loo. He's been using the 'john', as he insists on calling it, for most of our journey.

Do apples remind you of man's original sin? No? Me neither, but they are associated with Adam and Eve, aren't they? This apple on the *john* is Adam's, it's John *Adams*.

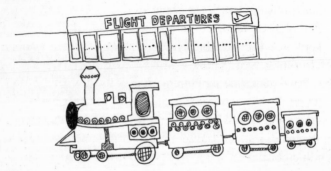

For *apple*, in other words, read *Adams*. So John Adams, an apple on the john, is our second president.

Well, this is good news: we've nearly arrived at the departures drop-off point outside the airport. You can see the taxi rank coming up on the right now.

But there's no space in the taxi rank, by the looks of things, because a huge train has gone and taken up every available spot. If I'm not mistaken, it's Thomas the Tank Engine.

We pull up behind the train, screeching to a halt, and clamber out on to the pavement with our bags.

He's quite a looker, this tank engine. He's covered in delicious fresh Jaffa cakes, just asking to be nibbled at. He's a *Thomas* with *Jaffas on: Thomas Jefferson*, the third president of the US.

We'll need some help with these bags of ours; that's the bare minimum we've come to expect after the limo ride. Good – here comes a porter with a trolley.

This guy reminds me of George Clooney off *ER*, but that might just be the medical uniform. And what's that in his belt? By golly – our medicine man, whoever he is, is carrying a massive black revolver.

The gun indicates that he's a *James*.

This is a little convention of ours. Think Jesse James or James Bond, both of whom enjoyed their guns, to nail this association – and for the rest of this walk, know that anyone carrying a **gun** is called **James**. Where there's a gun, we've got a James on our hands.

So who is this medicinal James, then? Well, he's *James Medicine* of course, or rather – *James Madison*. The gun-carrying medicine man next to Thomas, on the pavement, is the fourth US president, James Madison.

But, oh dear, there seems to be a problem.

Look over there by the revolving doors: a luscious woman – a dead ringer for Marilyn Monroe – has popped up and she's waving a brutal-looking revolver at us.

It's an alluring scenario – her skirts are billowing up, revealing soft white thighs; her perfume carries delightfully on the wind; she smells of peaches; her lips are in a mind-bending pout.

But what am I thinking? This is all irrelevant: she's pointing a gun at us!

That it's a Marilyn *Monroe* with a *gun* tells us that it's *James Monroe* holding us up here. A cheery hello, then, to James Monroe, the fifth president. And then let's get out of here; she's beginning to fire! She's taken down the doctor!

Dive in here, after me – into these revolving doors.

At least we're safe here, even if we do find ourselves jammed into a small triangular space with another piece of fruit on another stinking loo.

After John Adams, Washington's deputy, I'd rather thought I'd seen my last fruit on the john for the day.

This one at least looks a bit different to the last: yellower, more lumpen. I don't know if the reader knows what a

quince looks like, but it's basically just this: a yellow and lumpy variant on the apple. This here apple on the john strikes me, therefore, as a *quincy* apple, or, if we're to carry on calling **apples Adamses**, a *Quincy Adams*.

Indeed, this next president is called *John Quincy Adams*.

So, we've now met our first six US presidents.

George Washington was the shark, Jaws, washing himself tons while driving our limo. Our co-passenger, who was an apple sitting on the john, was John Adams. We were then forced to park in behind Thomas the Tank Engine with Jaffas on; that was Thomas Jefferson. As we sought a trolley, the Clooney-esque gun-toting medicine man to our right helped us out – he was James Madison – and we were trundling on our way to the doors of the departure hall when Marilyn Monroe stopped us in our tracks, waving another gun at us. That was James Monroe. We went it alone from there, escaping into the revolving door with the quincy apple on the loo, John Quincy Adams.

Emerging from the doors, we're going to need to pay a visit to that information desk you can see over there beneath the giant 'I' descending in yellow from the ceiling. It looks pretty user-friendly, this information point – it's nothing less than a converted ice-cream van.

Let's stroll over. But, wait a second, what's going on here? We're being queue-barged by a man moonwalking on his hands. His hands make the whishy-fist-whishy-fist-wishy-fist sound of a snake scuttling across the desert sands.

But this is the oldest trick in the book: he's facing as though he's leaving the queue, but his moonwalk moves take him to the front. Nobody suspects a thing, eh? I don't think so.

Yet who can really object to such gumption, style and technique?

And look at the man's huge hands! They could twiddle melons!

As if we need another reason to forgive him, you've got to admit he bears a striking resemblance to Michael Jackson. As far as I'm concerned, this hand-walking Jackson lookalike, this *Handrew Jackson*, is welcome to queue-barge as much as he pleases. Yes, you go on now, Handrew.

Andrew Jackson is our next president.

Things aren't going too well at our information desk.

For a start, the guy behind the window is a Martian. That's just not helpful.

Secondly, his van is burning, it reeks of barbecued alien flesh, and the flames are licking out of the top. The Martian's inhuman screams send a shiver down your spine.

I don't think we can get much sense from this *Martian in a van that's burning*, so we'll pass on from *Martin Van Buren*, the next president, to seek out our check-in desk by ourselves.

How on earth are we going to find it now?

But look – that guy there has got tickets for American Airlines; let's follow him, if only for the entertainment value. He is quite a sight: a wad of dollar bills hopping along with big bendy strides on little rubbery legs. He has his son in his arms and he's throwing him up and down in the air as they bumble along. The son's a disgusting-looking creature, a mangy featherless hen covered in green body hair.

Now wherever we have **dollar bills** think, well, Bill. Bill is a nickname for William, of course, so dollar bills stand in for **Williams**. Lock this in your mind, then: whenever you

see dollar bills, what you're really seeing is Williams.

So, our guide is a *William*, and his *hairy son* is a *hen*. So that makes him William (with a) Hen (for a) Hairy-son, or *William Henry Harrison* – our next president.

Rather kindly, Harrison lets us check in first, waving us past to the front of the queue.

There's just one person in front of us; he's at the check-in desk itself, having a fiery argument with the lady behind the counter, quite eye-catching in that polka-dot dress. We'll take a closer look at this woman in due course.

But what about the man! It's John Lennon, if I'm not mistaken – but there's no guitar in sight. Instead, he's checking in a whole bunch of bathroom tiles. They weigh a lot, these tiles, and this is the source of the argument. It seems that John will have to pay a surplus-baggage charge for them.

Disgusted at the very idea, he's decided instead to remove a few of the tiles from his luggage, and to decorate the front of the check-in desk. He's sticking them on now. This is terrific. The desk is being transformed by the fetching pink tile-work, a map of the US if I'm not mistaken.

This *John* who *tiles*, by the way, is *John Tyler*, our next president.

The lady behind the desk in her polka-dot dress, meanwhile, is not reacting kindly to this act of guerrilla decoration from Mr Tyler.

Well, look at her now! She's taken out a pistol and she's furiously firing it into the air, pausing between fusillades to poke John in the ribs. The bullets are K-shaped, which is pretty cool.

This woman, then, is a gun-slinger in a polka-dot dress who pokes her customers. Attention, please: she is *James* (for the gun) *K* (for the shape of its bullets) and *Polk* (for both the pokes and the polka-dot dress). After John Tyler, our next president is *James K Polk*.

As we check our own bags in, Polk has a piece of useful advice. Listen to this: we either 'look smart or get the treatment from security'.

Since we respect her dress sense, we'll take her advice seriously, and before we go through to the departure lounge, we'll now nip into the Tie Rack shop by the security passage. It's a typical airport shop – hundreds of ties arrayed in bright displays. Perfect. In we go.

But this is awesome! In the middle of the shop there's a quite wonderful scene: an entirely naked man, buttocks goose-pimpled in the cool of the air-conditioning, is having sugar poured over him by a gruff-looking shop assistant.

But it gets better.

As the sugar ripples over his body, it leaves in its wake a perfectly fitted suit. A double-breasted one, I'm afraid, but still incredible to see saccharine becoming suit.

This man who can do this, who is he?

The man who magically turns saccharine into suits is the legendary *saccharine tailor*. He's also known as *Zachary Taylor*, and he's the next president.

We pass to the back of the shop to try on some new clothes. But as we draw back the changing-room curtains . . . oh no, cover your eyes, this is truly monstrous.

I'm confronted by an expanse of lard here, rolls and rolls of it. An incredibly fat man, with a bucket at his side, is wedged on the bench at the back of the cubicle. I know it doesn't sound too bad, but I haven't told you the half of it. From the folds of his lard emerges a pipe with a tap at the end. His fat, a splutter of globular lard, is pouring out and splattering down into the bucket.

The guy's evidently having some kind of improvised liposuction. (And I never knew this, but human fat really stinks – of blue cheese, it seems. Close your nostrils as well.) He's following the level keenly as the bucket fills up with his fat. This is quite exciting; it's fast approaching the point marked 'Personal Best' on the side of the bucket.

There it goes! And listen up – the fat man's got an announcement to make:

'*Mi lard fill more*! Mi lard fill more! Mi lard fill more than ever before!'

I've no evidence with which to contradict this claim from *Millard Fillmore*, our next president.

So – that takes us to the end of the presidents who could be said to have worked out Jacksonian Democracy. We've seen them arranged all around the departures hall. Let's review them.

First, there was Andrew Jackson himself, the man who walked backwards but appeared to be going forward, and passed us on his hands on the way to the information van.

There we met Martin Van Buren, the Martian in that van that was burning.

We ended up making our way to check in with the help of a jumping wad of dollar bills and his hairy son, a hen. That was William Henry Harrison.

At the desk itself, a tiler who looked suspiciously like John Lennon was trying to check his tiles on to the plane, and was getting rid of the surplus by decorating the front of the check-in desk. This didn't impress the lady in the polka-dot dress, who poked at John Tyler with her gun firing K-shaped bullets; her name being James K Polk.

We took Polk's advice and went to Tie Rack to smarten ourselves up, but things were a little odd there.

First, there was the naked customer being dressed with a magic bag of sugar by Zachary Taylor, the saccharine tailor. Then there was the guy in the changing room at the back having his annual liposuction session and noticing how his lard filled more of the bucket than the previous year – that was Millard Fillmore.

Over all this time, Michael Jackson's greatest hits have been pumping out over the airport PA system. This has been the era of Jacksonian Democracy, after all.

Tremendous. We can now have a think about going

through security. Look serious, smarten yourselves up, post your shampoo back home – it'll only be confiscated otherwise. And get your tickets ready.

Or what?

Well, look here to the side of the queue to see what happens to people who don't obey the rules!

A Frenchman's been pierced clean through with a huge, sharpened baguette – and left hanging in midair. Unable to escape from this crusty prong, he just flails his arms and curses away in French.

'*Merde*,' says the *pierced Frenchie, Franklin Pierce*, our next president. All **Frenchmen** are called **Franklin** in this airport, I should stress. Make a note of it.

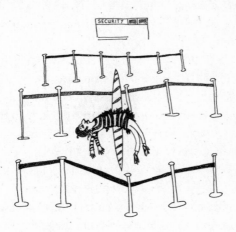

We're at the X-ray machine now, but the man in front of us seems engagingly unaware of the basic principles of aircraft security. If he puts that six-foot iron cannon of his through the machine, it'll be detected and then confiscated. Should we warn him?

Nah! Let's see what happens. This could be comic.

In he pops the cannon now, looking quite nonchalant as he saunters to the other end to collect it.

But what a shame – the X-ray man has spotted it and called security.

And our cannon smuggler's being muscled to the side to be interrogated by a bearded guard – let's listen in:

'Is this your cannon, sir?'

'It is.'

'Are you aware that no combat weapons are allowed on international flights?'

'I am, officer.' (Awkward pause.) 'But this isn't a very dangerous cannon, I promise. Let me show you.'

The passenger now presses a little button on the top of the cannon. As he does so, a plastic gun fires out on a spring from the end, and from the plastic gun a little flag with the word 'BOO' follows.

How extremely funny: it is a James – BOO – Cannon, a cannon that fires a gun (a James) from the end, that then goes 'BOO'. *James Buchanan* is the next president.

The chap charged with interviewing Buchanan doesn't seem at all amused, however. Get a load of that scowl!

He looks exactly like Abraham Lincoln, this security officer, and he has in his hands a rather extraordinary chain of bra-hams – hams wearing bras, linked all together in a circle like a lasso. They are *a bra-ham linkin'*. All in all, you can hardly quibble at my feeling that this next president is

Abraham Lincoln.

We have no bags with us, so all we have to do is go through the metal detector.

Passing through, however, it starts bleeping. And even removing our belt, keys and nose rings won't stop it going off. It looks like they're going to have to call out the body-search team.

Let's hope it's no one we know; that would be *so* embarrassing.

An incredibly tall security official, Abraham Lincoln's deputy, duly steps forward.

And, bless my soul, I think we do know him! But it's all right – we don't know him personally, just by reputation.

It's Magic Johnson, the basketball star!

Oh my God, look at the size of his hands! They're absolutely vast!

Whooooah! Magic Johnson lifts us off the ground now, and, in a single movement, he's searched the entire surface of our body.

How? He's rolled us back and forth like a tubule of Play-Doh between his palms. That felt like a spell in a tumble dryer.

Fortunately, he can't find any weapons, this hands-on Johnson character (this 'Handrew' Johnson) and he drops us dizzily back to ground level.

Andrew Johnson, Magic Johnson with big hands, is the next president after Lincoln.

We're just about through now; it only remains for us to have our passports checked. Approaching the booth, it sounds as if two bears are mating inside.

But when we get close enough to see, it's clearly just a man in military uniform singing, or rather grunting, the US national anthem. No words, just the notes, grunted in the bass register: an unusual way to perform the 'Star-spangled Banner', but very moving.

This military man who emits grunts, who grunts his way through the US national anthem – he's US Grunt, or Ulysses S Grant.

Now, let's quickly review this last sequence. First we had the Frenchman of whom an example had been made in the run-up to the X-ray machine. He'd been totally pierced by a sharpened baguette. He was Franklin Pierce. Then there was James Buchanan having a bit of fun with security with his BOO-cannon. Abraham Lincoln, manning the X-ray machines, didn't seem that amused by Buchanan's antics, and interrogated him. The linkin' bra-hams were the least intimidating part, I'd say.

Then we ran into problems as we got bleeped passing through the metal detector; Magic Johnson with huge hands, Andrew Johnson that is, gave us a full body search.

After that ordeal, we were able to proceed to passport control, where Ulysses S Grant was having such an amusing time grunting his way through the US national anthem.

So we're finally through and free to enjoy the departure lounge. First things first: let's have ourselves a bit of duty free.

And look – excellent news. There's a shop just over there in front of us.

Despite being only twenty yards away, it looks like it's going to be a difficult one to reach: a haze of bees is buzzing, in front of us blocking our way to duty free. Maybe we should chuck in the idea of getting us some tax-free produce.

But wait a second – there's an innovative ferryman just here, providing a crossing service. He's added a rudder to a standard Ford automobile, and he's offering lifts across the bee haze.

We get into the ruddered Ford and cross the bee haze. And this man with a *ruddered Ford* for the *bee haze*? He's actually *Rutherford B Hayes*, our next president.

Having forded the bees, we trample ashore just short of the duty-free emporium. Fantastically, outside the doors they've got a prize raffle for one of those delicious cars, a Jaguar – check the way it spins round on the revolving stage.

The Jag is being pretend-driven by an actor dressed up as Garfield the cat. You haven't quite reached the top of the career ladder, have you, if you find yourself dressed as a cat in an airport. Whoops – did I say that out loud? Yes, I did, and Garfield's angrily whipped out a pair of guns!

Good God, I think he means to

kill us . . . he's firing at us through the windscreen! Quick – let's dive into the duty-free shop.

Phew. That was a close shave. Who on earth does that guy think he is?

Safely inside, catching our breath, we can work out that the guns obviously mean he thinks he's a James. A James Garfield, presumably, what with the outfit. And the car's got to be a clue too: JAG, these are surely his initials. So, all in all, it must be *James A Garfield*.

James A Garfield in his Jag marks the transition into a new phase in the presidency, known as the Golden Era. And how appropriate that this duty-free emporium should be advertised with the (misleading) caption 'Gold in here!'

We are now standing inside at the end of a long aisle running off to the right, parallel to the shop windows.

But, before we go down the aisle, look, directly in front of us, right beyond the doors . . . there is the most enormous chest of oak and iron. What is a chest doing here? Could it be full of treasure?

Why don't you lean over and get a closer look? Go on, stop looking shy. Why not try and open it?

Pow!

Whoops – sorry! I had no idea the lid would fly open so suddenly, whacking you on the chin like that. At least the floor's a good spot from which to watch this amazing burst of light, and the not unholy vision of King Arthur, jack-in-the-box, looming above us.

Before we know it, though, Arthur has disappeared, the

chest closing so suddenly that the bang leaves a ringing sound in the ears.

In summary, then, that wasn't a chest of treasure at all, but rather *a chest o' Arthur* or *Chester Arthur*, the next president.

I must say that I do enjoy a bit of interior foliage. Too few people keep lawns in their sitting rooms, too few lemon trees dangle over beds; there's too much wallpaper in this world and not enough ivy, don't you think?

But this here aisle, a glorious avenue of trees, pleases me greatly.

These trees, interestingly, have meat cleavers growing from their branches, glinting viciously in the light. This aisle is a grove of cleavers.

It represents *Grover Cleveland*, does this *grove o' cleavers*, who was the president following Chester Arthur.

And now something unique in American presidential history occurs: in the middle of this president, in the middle of this grove, there is another president. In other words, Grover Cleveland's spell as president is interrupted; he serves on two non-consecutive occasions.

Who is the man in the middle, who surely deserves as

much credit as Cleveland for having helped him achieve this famous feat?

We can see him clearly in the centre of the grove of cleavers, bending over what looks to be his son, a terrifically hairy young boy.

What's he bending over this unusual infant for, you may ask?

Well, the answer is that he's *bending* to pour *jam into* his *hairy son*.

What?

You see – his name is *Ben jam in Harri son*; he's *bending to put jam into his hairy son*. Benjamin Harrison is our next president.

Treading softly past so as not to disturb him, we of course enjoy a second stint in the grove of cleavers, Grover Cleveland.

The shelves have been very helpfully labelled to stave off confusion. The labels on the aisle read Grover Cleveland, Benjamin Harrison, Grover Cleveland.

Harrison, by the way, is the grandson of the chap who helped us find check-in, the guy made of dollar bills juggling a hairy hen who turned out to be his son: William Henry Harrison.

Excellent work. We've now got to the end of the aisle, and

since there's nothing worth buying here we may as well make a quick stop at the currency-exchange booth and then head straight to the departure gate.

There's one just next door to the duty-free emporium. Let's go get us some dollars.

Hey you! Come back! I wouldn't queue-barge an animal like that, sunshine. Come back and join us in the line

behind, or you'll find yourself stampeded!

The mucky animal already exchanging some money at the booth looks kind enough, but one never can tell, you know.

It's Nelly the Elephant (the one who packed her trunk and said goodbye to the circus). But, dear me, since leaving the circus, she's become terribly mucky; she's really plastered in muck.

She is a mucky Nelly, or, for short, mucky N'ly. For even shorter, she's a McKinley. And with all these dollar bills she's just acquired for her holiday, she'll become a William McKinley. She now drops them all on the floor and rolls around, so that the bills stick in the muck all over her, covering her completely.

It really couldn't be clearer that this is *William mucky N'lly*, or *William McKinley*.

Once President McKinley's finished, we can get our own money. As we hand over our notes to be changed, we see that the chap behind the counter is a teddy bear dressed in a loose felt suit.

A *teddy* dressed in *loose felt*? This must be Teddy Roosevelt. Teddy is short for Theodore, and it's true that *Theodore* also has *the odour* of a teddy – *the ador*-able odour

83

one associates with attics and grandparents.

Anyhow, Theodore Roosevelt slides us over a wad of dollar bills and we're good to roll.

So, for a bit of a recap: we headed into the Golden Era of American history in a ruddered-Ford ride through the bee haze with Rutherford B Hayes. In the Jag outside the duty-free shop we saw James A Garfield, a gun-toting variant on Garfield the cat.

Inside the misleadingly advertised 'Gold in here!' duty-free emporium, we first met King Arthur emerging from his chest, that was Chester A Arthur. Next we walked the length of the grove of cleavers – Grover Cleveland – in the middle of which we noticed the presence of a man bending to put jam in his hairy son. That was Benjamin Harrison, the guy dividing Grover Cleveland's two terms. So the aisle went Cleveland, Harrison, Cleveland.

Emerging from the duty-free emporium, we went next door to get some foreign currency. William McKinley was the mucky Nelly with dollar bills stuck all over, and the teddy bear behind the counter was Teddy Roosevelt, which we knew from his loose felt suit.

Now, then: our flight's quite soon, so we need to be off to the departure gate. Let me have a quick look at the tickets. Oh, how typical! We're leaving from gate number seventy something. We're going to need to take the airport monorail shuttle.

The doors to the shuttle aren't far and the board says we'll just have to wait a couple of minutes for the next train.

Extraordinary. Wooden garden hoes litter the floor in

front of the doors to the monorail. Er, hello? Health hazard? I know from bitter experience that to step on a hoe is to have its handle fly up and pong you on the nose.

Look – this is exactly what I'm talking about – an exceptionally fat wad of dollar bills is walking busily towards the doors. He'd better look where he's going if he wants to keep that nose intact.

The first wooden hoe (the first hoe-wood, so to speak) is catapulted up by his foot and rattles into his snout. Ouch.

Confused, he carries on towards the doors, trying to escape a phantom assailant.

The next hoe-wood hits him even harder, going *splang* into his now bloodied face.

But he's panicking, picking up speed now.

Poosh! Thwack! Plonk!

This is utterly *daft*. This *William*, this wad of dollar bills who keeps stepping on *hoe-woods*, must be William Hoe-wood Daft, or *William Howard Taft*.

William Howard Taft is our next president.

Finally – the doors are opening, and we can enter the shuttle. But this is no public-spirited way to use a cramped monorail carriage: a tennis player is taking up a whole row of the seats with all his wooden Wilson tennis racquets.

This unhelpful sportsman has a *wood-row of Wilsons*; in fact, he is called *Woodrow Wilson*. And he's our next president.

Let's go and sit at the front of the train, well away from this man with his wood-row of Wilsons.

Hmm . . . Is it just me or do your feet feel a little heavy?

Suspiciously so. Urrgh. The whole floor of the train is thick with a layer of slowly hardening glue.

And this is interesting – there are lots of live rabbits on the floor that appear to be struggling, in this hardening glue, to unstick themselves.

Indeed, on considering the matter, you have to think that this whole warren's worth of rabbits has become irretrievably stuck. They'll probably miss their flights. A

warren (scuppered by a) *glue* that's *hardening* – Warren Glue Hardening – should make us think of *Warren G Harding*, the next president.

Thank goodness we've arrived at our stop. The doors open and first through them, and on to the escalator beyond, is a swaggering fridge.

Watch how, vainly, he turns to face us so that we can all get a good view of his hard white body and designer underwear.

The man's name is Calvin Koolidge, this cooling fridge who wears Calvin Klein underwear. And *Calvin Coolidge* is our next president.

At the top of the escalator (this is just *soooo* exciting) we're just yards away from the first-class lounge. Yes, I did say first class. Oh yes.

Carbon footprint, schmarbon footprint.

Talking of footprints, we'll be making some soon: the ground running up to the lounge's glass doors is covered in sherbet. Fizzletastic!

Unfortunately, there is an airport worker doing his best to hoover it all up. This man is Herbert Hoover. He *hoovers up sherbet*, that's how we know. *Herbert Hoover* is the president after Calvin Coolidge.

Good. Let's revise our last bunch of presidents, then.

After we'd got our cash from Theodore Roosevelt, we saw that daft wad of dollar bills standing on wooden hoes: William Howard Taft. In the train, we met two presidents: the chap with the row of wooden Wilson tennis racquets – that was Woodrow Wilson – and then the hardening glue that had trapped a warren's worth of rabbits to the floor – that was Warren G Harding.

First off the train was the cool fridge with the designer underwear, he was Calvin Coolidge. And immediately at the top of the escalator was the president we just met hoovering up sherbet. That was Herbert Hoover.

We're doing splendidly, and we're on the finishing straight.

Return your mind to our present location at the top of the escalator, and follow me as I tread my way over the sherbet.

Make sure to shut the glass door into the lounge behind the last of you and then take a moment to admire the scene.

It's properly cool, this. Presidentially so. There are all sorts of goodies here.

The best thing of all, perhaps, is that this lounge has a snooker table. And there's a game going on. Let's check it out.

A Frenchman's on cue. He's got a terrific beret, and he's just breaking now, having placed the ball on the D. *Thwhack!*

Well, this is remarkable. He pots without making contact.

The table, you see, has got incredibly loose felt all over it. The ball goes whizzing over the surface and, even though it misses all the other balls, the waves it sends rippling over the cloth manage to force a red into the pocket. Sweet.

This Frenchman is a Franklin, of course. But that's not his full name. The loose felt surface of his snooker table tells us that he must be *Franklin Loose-felt*, or, rather, Roosevelt.

So this Franklin playing from the D on a loose-felt table is *Franklin D Roosevelt*, our next president.

But things keep getting better in this lounge. Look, over there, an incredibly hairy man is playing at a piano next to the bar.

His hair is gleaming white because he keeps lots of chewing gum in it – he plays a four-hour set, after all, and needs to sustain himself.

Who is this man who chews his own hair? He is the hairy-chew man and he's happy to confirm this for us. 'It's true, man,' he says. 'I'm the hairy-chew man.'

Harry Chewman, or, rather, *Truman*, is our next president. A man who chews on the gum he keeps in his hair: a hairy-chew man.

We leave him to tinkle away on his piano and move on to the bar. Drinks are free here, apparently. And since the first rule of life for economic man is never to pass over a freebie we'll be getting stuck in. Oh yes.

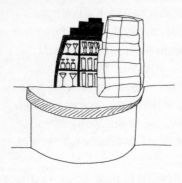

On the bar, there's a great big ice sculpture, a kind of white ice tower, if you will. It's rather beautiful.

And when we quiz the barman he tells us that this isn't just any old white ice tower – it is '*dee* white ice tower'. Or Dwight Eisenhower, if we prefer. *Dee white ice tower* of *Dwight Eisenhower* is our next president.

We settle down right by the boarding desk in the corner with an iced cocktail to hand. (Obtained by pouring a bottle over Dwight Eisenhower and collecting the ice-cold liquid that trickled to the bottom. Lush.)

We're waiting for the announcement that we can board our flight.

A deafening crackle, and the PA system bursts into action. 'The flight to JFK International is now boarding . . .'

Passengers with special tickets get to go first. No, don't sigh and complain; we're among the passengers who possess such tickets. Ha!

Pushing to the front of the queue, we hand ours over to the steward behind the ticket machine. And, since JFK is a very personable airport, they've actually sent JFK himself to inspect our tickets. A very handsome man, and what a pleasure to have *John F Kennedy* himself taking such care over proceedings!

'Is it true, President Kennedy, that you won a Pulitzer Prize?' we ask him.

'Yes,' he responds, but there's no more time for chat; people are waiting.

John F Kennedy thus waves us through and down the enclosed ramp towards the vehicle idling on the tarmac, waiting to take us to our plane. This ramp is lined on both

sides with Boris Johnsons who are saluting us in a most amusing fashion.

It's *lined by B Johnsons*?

Yes, it is.

They're saluting?

Some of them.

Then this ramp must be President *Lyndon B Johnson*.

Indeed.

And here's another surprise. Descending from the tunnel on to the tarmac, we clatter straight into Richard Gere.

'Look where you're going, pretty boy,' we say to him, adopting a friendly tone in the hope he'll introduce us one day to Julia Roberts.

Richard smiles thinly, but looks uncomfortable.

And I can see why – he's got a little boy under his arm. And listen to the boy crying out. He blubbers, 'Richard, don't steal me! I'm somebody's son.'

But *Richard* with a *nicked son* won't let our unexpected arrival scupper his well-laid plans. Turning on his heels, he sprints for the nearby car, intending to throw the nicked son in the boot. He fails, for reasons we'll go into another time.

Richard nicking a son: *Richard Nixon*, our next president.

Great, now that's over with we can climb into the wonderful golden Ford that's been laid on to ferry us to the plane. It's the same one that Nixon recently failed to thrust the nicked son into.

Take a look at this marvellous open-top machine, gleaming beautifully in the sunshine in front of us. The best feature, surely, is the comedy red nose that's been stapled on to the bonnet.

It reminds us of Rudolph the Red-nosed Reindeer. A *gold Ford* with *Rudolph*'s nose in the middle of the bonnet must be being driven by G(era)ld Rudolph Ford, if I'm not mistaken.

Hello, *Gerald R Ford*!

It's not long till our flight takes off! Let's go!

Urrgh. But why are we slowing down so soon? We seem to be having tyre problems . . . and, look, who's this taking advantage, shooting past us on the right-hand side?

He appears to be on an electric cart. Yes, you can see the distinctive golf-buggy shape, he's definitely an e-carter, this person overtaking us.

And, what's more, he's carrying a sawn-off shotgun. Oh please don't shoot us, whoever you are!

Wait a second. Guns are Jameses, carters drive carts and anything electronic these days begins with an e. Could this be President *James E Carter*, this man with a gun in an e-cart?

It certainly could. James E Carter is the president overtaking, or rather taking over from, Gerald R Ford.

The e-cart is now well in front; he's gunning for the best seats, the cad.

Stay calm, people! A member of the American Airlines staff, who's seen this violent overtaking manoeuvre from the plane, no doubt, has emerged with a large and futuristic weapon in his hands. Hurrah for Ronald McDonald and his ray-gun!

Look at those great blue electrical flames that now leap from the nozzle of the ray-gun.

Glorious justice! Ronald has stunned the e-carter, who has – *crunch!* – nobbled his buggy on the steps of the plane. That'll give Carter something to think about.

And this *Ronald* with a *ray-gun* is presumably *Ronald Reagan*, our next president.

After we've picked our way over the ruins of Carter's presidency at the foot of the steps, Reagan ushers us up into the plane. This is pretty cool: check out the cockpit – the captain's door has been left open, revealing all those dials and flashing lights. Why don't we go say hi to the pilots?

Why not indeed?

In the pilot's seat, that's the one on the right, sits a large shark. When I say seat, by the way, what I really mean is a

bush, for the shark (it's *Jaws* again, by the looks of things) evidently likes to pilot his plane while seated in a large *bush*. What kind of bush, you might ask? Well, it seems to be a *sherbet bush* – there are packets of sherbet all over it.

Our pilot is George (Jaws) Herbert (sherbet) Bush (bush).

And who is the co-pilot, sitting to the left of *George H Bush*? I'm pretty sure we can recognize this one: it's Bill Clinton. In case you don't know him, let me describe the guy. He resembles a very shiny set of dollar bills: some bills that are a glintin' in the light. *Bills glintin'* fairly accurately describes *Bill Clinton*. Bill Clinton is the president after Bush the elder.

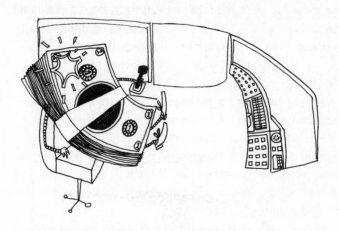

But, oh dearie me, look who else has just entered the
cockpit! The stewardess has arrived with a small shark, who
is asking whether he can sit on the pilot's knee and drive the
plane.

'I want to have a go!' cries the
mini-shark.

This little boy has a large W
on his shirt – and I do believe
that he's our pilot's son. The boy
resembles his father, I'd say, in
almost all respects except that he's
much smaller and knows much
less about controlling an aircraft.

But it seems the elder shark is
a very indulgent parent, for he
now vacates the bush and, despite
almost everyone's objections, he
invites the little boy to have a go at
piloting the plane through take-off.

So *George W Bush*, a miniature

Jaws with a W on his T-shirt, and now sitting on the bush, assumes the controls and off we go. You'll need to hold on tight. George W Bush is the last president on this list, and we're now well and truly off to America!

Just in case you have any uncertainties remaining, let's take a look over our whole presidential journey, right from the very beginning.

We began in a limo that was piloted by a Jaws washing himself – George Washington; facing us in the back, we had an apple on the passenger loo, or 'john'. The next president, then, was John Adams, since apples are associated with the biblical Adam.

We unloaded behind a Thomas the Tank Engine with Jaffas on, and it was next to this Thomas Jefferson that we met James Madison, the gun-wielding medicine man, and saw the beginnings of the fire fight he had with the luscious James Monroe, with her iconic, billowing skirts.

In the revolving doors into the airport, we were squeezed in with John Quincy Adams, a quince-like apple on another john, and we then headed for the information van opposite. On the way, we were delighted to be queue-barged by the king of pop moonwalking on his hands, Andrew Jackson.

Not that it mattered, anyhow: the Martian in the van that was burning, Martin Van Buren, was totally incapable of telling us anything coherent.

Lucky we found William Henry Harrison, the wad of dollar bills with his hairy son, to take us to the American Airlines check-in desk.

There we saw John Tyler tiling the front of the desk in pink. He was being served, as we were too, by a polka-dot-dressed lady, who fired K-shaped bullets from her gun: that was James K. Polk.

We took her advice and headed to Tie Rack to pick up

some better clothes. There, we saw the amazing saccharine tailor, Zachary Taylor, and after him the lardy serial liposuctioning man, who boasted 'mi lard fill more'. That was Millard Fillmore.

On to security, where Jacko's music (and with it Jacksonian Democracy) was no longer being played, but rather an atmosphere of conflict was building up.

First Franklin Pierce, the Frenchman, was pierced by a sharpened baguette. Then, at the X-ray machine, was James Buchanan: he was arrested for his silliness by the iconic Abraham Lincoln (whose bra-hams were linkin').

Andrew 'Magic' Johnson searched us with his enormous hands after we subsequently bleeped the metal detector, and we then had that amusing experience of having our passports stamped by Ulysses S Grant, who grunted his way through the US national anthem.

Before we reached the Golden Era, our last test was to pass through that bee haze, which we did by fording it in a ruddered Ford. The boatman was Rutherford B Hayes.

Outside the duty-free emporium, at the other end of the bee haze, we saw James A Garfield in his Jag. When he shot at us, we ran into the shop. There, our attention was grabbed by the presence of a large chest, which flipped open to reveal King Arthur. He and his trunk were Chester A Arthur – a chest of an Arthur.

Into a grove o' cleavers next – in the middle of which we found a man bending to pour jam into his hairy son, Benjamin Harrison. He was the president who divided Grover Cleveland's two terms in office.

After leaving the emporium, we went to change some money, and found that mucky Nelly at the exchange booth, covered in dollar bills: that was William McKinley. He was being served by the odorous teddy dressed in loose felt: that was Theodore 'Teddy' Roosevelt.

By now it was time for the monorail to the departure gate. Waiting for the train's doors to open, we saw another wad of dollar bills, this one daftly wandering in a field of wooden hoes, getting himself whacked relentlessly on the nose. That was William Howard (hoe-wood) Taft.

Inside the train, there was Woodrow Wilson of course, the chap selfishly hogging a row of seats for his wooden Wilson tennis racquets, and at the very front of the carriage we found a warren of rabbits stuck in hardening glue. That was Warren G Harding.

We can zoom from here to the end, because we're good at the last bit.

Calvin Coolidge was the fridge looking cool on the escalator; Herbert Hoover was the man hoovering up the sherbet at the top. Inside the first-class lounge, Franklin D Roosevelt was playing snooker on his loose-felt table and we met that hairy-chew man, the guy who chewed his own hair. He was playing piano near dee white ice-tower: Harry S Truman and Dwight Eisenhower. And we were soon on the move again, past JFK and that line of B Johnsons (Lyndon B Johnson) down to Richard Gere, criminally trying to nick someone's son and hide him in a golden Ford car. That was Richard Nixon and, after, Gerald Ford.

We enjoyed our lift from Gerald Ford and even though we were overtaken by the gun-handling electric carter, we still got on to the plane first, because James E Carter was zapped by Ronald Reagan's ray-gun from the plane's steps.

An instant later and we were in the cockpit, where we saw Jaws in his pilot's bush of sherbet – George Herbert Bush – and Bill Clinton in the second pilot's seat. It was only right at the end, with George H Bush's mini-shark son taking the controls, that we actually ran back to take our seats for take-off.

I can't see our neighbour here, he's bending over to pick

something off the floor. But I can, at the least, give you an indication of his appearance: he resembles at once a barracuda and a barmaid.

ROUND TWO: SPOTTING THE DETAIL

So you know the presidents now. To make absolutely sure, you can flick your way through the pictures we've had so far.

What follows is a second pass over the events of the walk. This time, since we know more or less what happens in broad outline, we're going to attend a little more to the details. We're going to see what each president got up to. Let's go on our way without further delay.

1

Take a look, first of all, at **George Washington**, our limo-driving shark who's dressed as a farmer. See how he holds a map, which he's gradually revolving because it's upside down. And on the dashboard, all of his unopened bills and admin, piled up willy-nilly.

The map is actually a battle plan from the Revolutionary War, where Washington led the Continental Forces. These letters are America's admin, not his, as it turns out. He left his farm to become president, and sorted out the country's debt, banking and taxation.

2

Amusing himself in the back of the limo we still have **John Adams**, the apple on the john. Note how the limo's interior is done up in white leather: Adams was the first president to live in the White House.

And look, our apple's listening to 'Revolution' by the Beatles on a borrowed iPod. This reminds us of how Adams borrowed the money necessary to fund the Revolutionary War.

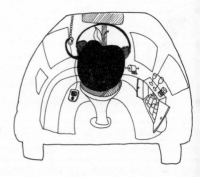

3   Once we're out on the pavement, we can take a closer look at **Thomas Jefferson**, our Thomas the Tank Engine with Jaffas on, who is reading the *Independent* newspaper: he was, of course, the principal author of the Declaration of Independence.

And look – there's a parrot called *Polly* doing *maths* on his funnel, working out the combined cost of *Lois* Lane and *Anna* Kournikova.

Jefferson was famously a great polymath and the defining moment of his presidency was the Louisiana Purchase (Lois and Anna), where the US acquired, effectively, the whole middle third of its current-day territory.

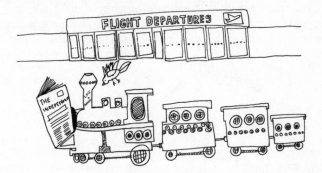

4   To the side of the train, **James Madison**, our gun-toting medicine man, isn't actually being that much help with our bags – his trolley's already full up with a vast copy of the American Constitution, of which he was the principal author.

When Madison gets shot by Monroe (which didn't happen by the way) make sure you hear how he says in a Darth Vader voice, 'I am your father, or at least the last of them.'

For Madison was, eventually, the last of the founding fathers to die.

And, forgive me for bringing family lore in at this point, but it was during Madison's presidency that the War of 1812 took place. Despite its name, this war lasted right through 1814, when your author's great-great-great-uncle raided Washington and burnt down the White House. His name was Admiral Cockburn. So imagine a burning cockerel on Madison's shoulder saying to him, 'I burnt your house down at fourteen minutes past six, how do you like that?' And imagine how this must nearly have brought on an epileptic seizure. That'll remind you that Madison was epileptic.

101

5 **James Monroe** is outside the revolving doors. Take another look at her skirts billowing up. Doesn't that give you good feelings? Monroe's presidency was known as the 'Era of Good Feelings' for its economic prosperity and social peace. And why are Monroe's skirts blowing up like this?

Well, look to the pavement! A steam boat is chugging past, puffing up her skirts with its plume of steam. Monroe was the first president to ride a steam boat.

And, by the way, when Marilyn shoots the doc, that's the Monroe doctorin', or Monroe Doctrine, that historians get so excited about.

6

If we look again at **John Quincy Adams** in the revolving doors, we can see that he's stark naked and soaking wet: he's been skinny dipping again in the Potomac River. Adams once even gave an interview to a female journalist while the pair skinny dipped.

In the segment of the revolving doors in front, there's a crowd of intelligent-looking schoolboys, who he's trying to force through this *ingress* into the departures hall. But the boys are all getting stuck; he can't push them through. The historical Adams was similarly unable to get his ambitious programme of educational reform through *congress*.

And how astonishingly shiny he is! He must be very keen indeed on *a polishin'*. That'll be because he was an early proponent of *abolishin'* slavery – and cleaning up America's conscience.

7

From this position we can see the beginning of **Andrew Jackson**'s moonwalk. It actually starts from a log cabin – entirely appropriate, since he was the first president born in a log cabin.

As he walks out, all of the people nearby begin grooving around and even indulging in a bit of 'wreckage' (of, among other things, banks), inspired by his excellent moves: just like at his legendary inauguration party, where his mates from Tennessee got so out of control that the White House was trashed, and the president had to escape to a nearby hotel, where he no doubt plotted the (ultimately unsuccessful) closure of the National Bank in peace. Notice that the ground across which he moonwalks is strewn with thirteen *jewels*; a hot-tempered president, Jackson fought thirteen *duels* in his eventful life.

8   When **Martin Van Buren**, our Martian in the information van, caught fire, the time was exactly 18:37 hours. It's worth taking a look at the scenes of panic – this being so similar to the famous *Panic of 1837*, which took place during Van Buren's presidency.

He instructs everyone to calm down in Dutch – telling them that he, like them, is American. Van Buren, who grew up in a Dutch-speaking (Martian) community, was the only president not to speak English as a first language. But he was also the first president born an American citizen.

9

During the second pass over our meeting with **William Henry Harrison**, we notice that he is actually comprised of sixty-eight one-dollar bills. He took office at the age of sixty-eight too, and was thus the oldest president to take office (till Ronald Reagan, 140 years later).

On the way over to the check-in desk, he insists on telling us the entirety of his insanely long postal address. At the moment he completes this long address, he collapses with exhaustion and dies – just next to Tyler. This reminds you of the way the historical William Henry Harrison died just a month into his presidency, from pneumonia, caught during his absurdly long inaugural address.

10

At our second visit to the check-in desk itself we hear how **John Tyler**, our tiling John Lennon, has been upgraded! Because of a sudden vacancy, he's been bumped from second to first class, from vice-president to president. He celebrates by adding a new area to the map of the US he's been tiling on to the front of the desk. It's Texas, which was indeed added to the Union during Tyler's presidency, to which he was upgraded after his predecessor's unfortunate death.

11 **James K Polk**, leaning over bustily in her polka-dot dress from behind the desk, now adds some tiles of her own, extending the map all the way to the West Coast of the continent. California was among the western states added to the Union during Polk's presidency.

And she now responds to our question too, about why she is a woman. It turns out that she is actually Polk's wife, deputizing for him. Polk ran the country as a double act with his wife, Sarah, who attended cabinet meetings with him and shared in much of his decision-making.

12

Over in the Tie Rack, **Zachary Taylor**, our magical saccharine tailor, always hums (in the major key), and is actually so short, if you look at him, that he needs a stool to be able to reach above his customer and pour. His horse, which bears a close resemblance to Whitney Houston, is grazing just outside the Tie Rack on some lawn. Its saddle has slipped on to its flank.

Taylor was a famously short soldier, ranked major, who always rode side-saddle into battle, and kept his old war-horse, Whitney, on the White House lawn.

13

Millard Fillmore, our incredibly fat man in the changing-booth having his yearly liposuction, is being aided by a servant with dentures, we can now see, who is wiping the edge of the bucket with a cloth.

This may remind us that Millard Fillmore was an indentured servant (a kind of contracted slave) who'd previously made cloths.

14

Passing through security next, we meet **Franklin Pierce**, our pierced Frenchman; he is, if you look closely at him, an easy-going, good-looking and successful lawyer. Basically, a male version of Calista Flockhart from *Ally McBeal*. Can you not see the similarity?

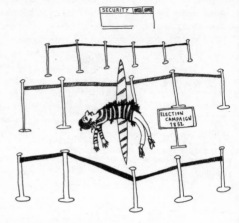

He's not making any speeches or doing anything really, except being pierced. What a way to campaign! It causes him to slide down the piercing baguette towards the ground. He's experiencing a landslide. History tells us that Pierce didn't make a speech, let alone do a campaign rally, and yet won a landslide election victory.

15

James Buchanan, our joker putting the cannon through the X-ray machine, has so freaked out a fellow passenger called Caroline, the winner of this year's Miss Carolina pageant, no less, that she's just leapt the barrier and is making a dash for safety.

This scene is curiously linked to the events of Buchanan's disastrous presidency, which saw Carolina and other Southern states 'breaking from the Union' – running off and declaring independence.

That's the thing about practical jokes – not everyone finds them funny. No wonder that Buchanan was a life-long bachelor.

With so many passengers breaking rank, it'll be left to the security man to sort this all out.

16

Abraham Lincoln, our six-foot-four security man, soon gathers back together all the passengers by lassoing them with his linkin' bra-hams, muttering at them about the cause.

Just so, the historical Lincoln, the tallest president at six feet and four inches, led the army in the Civil War and quashed the attempts of the South to break away from the North (over the 'question' of slavery). He mutters because that's what martyrs do in this book, and Lincoln became a martyr for the anti-slavery cause when he was assassinated in 1865.

17

On the other side of our walk-through metal detector **Andrew Johnson**, our body-searching Magic Johnson, finds some cash in our pocket and asks to borrow it. As he does so, his dentures clatter out on to the ground. Revolting.

This may remind us that, like Fillmore, Johnson was an indentured servant, and so poor when he became president that he needed to borrow money to get his things to the White House.

We punish the basketballer for his cheek – by slam-dunking a peach on to his lofty scalp. Johnson was the first president impeached.

18

Passing on through to the passport booth we re-encounter **Ulysses S Grant**, our anthem-grunting passport man, who's wearing a full general's uniform. And his booth is covered in posters of Victoria Beckham advertising hamburgers. This is all very odd.

But then Grant was the top Civil War general, whose campaign of Vick's-burger, or Vicksburg, is still admired for its brilliance by military historians today.

He stamps vinegar into our passports with a cucumber. This reminds one how Grant liked to have cucumbers soaked in vinegar for breakfast.

19

The bee haze over which **Rutherford B Hayes** boats makes a most extraordinary humming sound. On listening to it a second time we hear that it's humming 'California Dreaming'. Hayes was, incidentally, the first president to visit California.

If you're wondering why we are crossing this haze of bees in a Ford with a rudder and not that railroad bridge you can see over to the left, the reason is that there's been a railroad strike. The railroad strike (of 1877) was one of the defining moments of Hayes's presidency.

20

Beyond the bee haze in front of the duty-free emporium, **James A Garfield**, turns out to be interrupting his own sermon (delivered in Latin) to shoot out like this. But not at us – he is returning fire to the assassin who'll kill him.

This may help us remember that Garfield was an evangelist preacher, and the only ever such to become president. He spoke Latin and Greek, and his shooting with two hands reminds us that he was ambidextrous.

21

Passing into the duty-free emporium, we meet **Chester A Arthur** again. King Arthur really does shine astonishingly brightly. This is surely linked to his suffering from Bright's disease, a disorder of the kidneys.

And look how he's got a massive weight, a ton at least, on a kind of pendulum that he's jiggling about in a very civilized fashion.

This may remind us of his pendulum-ton, or rather Pendle-ton Reform Act, with which he re-jigged the civil service.

22

Grover Cleveland, our grove of meat-cleavers, was, as we know, the only US president to have been elected on two non-consecutive occasions. You may notice Babe Ruth, the baseball player, practising his game in Grover Cleveland's grove of cleavers, hitting home runs, straight and true, over and over. Cleveland, you see, had had a baby called Ruth – after whom Nestlé named a drink 'Baby Ruth'. And his presidential style was distinguished by its straightforwardness and honesty.

23

Benjamin Harrison, in the middle of the grove, has taken off his Indian headdress to pour jam into his son's mouth. He's from Indiana. He's telling his hairy son that he's worth a billion dollars – speaking very clearly so that, when he's old enough to understand, his son can listen to the recording Harrison's making.

What does this all tell us? That Harrison presided over the first administration to spend a billion dollars and that he was the first president to have their voice recorded.

24

Grover Cleveland, our grove of meat-cleavers, was , as we know, the only US President to have been elected on two non-consecutive occasions. Well done him! Make sure you drill that Cleveland-Harrison-Cleveland combo deep into your mind.

25

At the currency-exchange window, **William McKinley**, our mucky Nelly, has a massive advertising hoarding atop: McKinley was the first to use sophisticated advertising techniques in a presidential campaign. He's campaigning on the old Spanish-American War ticket.

And did I mention that McKinley, this elephant, is minute – just five foot four, and the smallest US president, despite being an elephant? Or that she will be assassinated by that big-game hunter stalking up behind her?

26

Teddy Roosevelt, our teddy in a loose-felt suit behind the counter, is a proud little schoolboy, just four stones and two pounds heavy, with a medal round his neck. He's won this medal for exchanging Russian for Japanese notes and vice-versa.

Which suggests all this: that he became the youngest ever president at age forty-two, and won the Nobel Peace Prize for negotiating the end to the Russo-Japanese War.

27

Over by the doors to the monorail, **William Howard Taft**, his wad-bod looking immensely fat, isn't just treading on hoe-woods, he's upsetting games of monopoly too: family games being played among the hoes. He remains utterly peaceful despite the repeated blows to his face.

Taft, America's fattest ever president, devoted himself to busting monopolies and pursuing peace.

28

Inside the train, **Woodrow Wilson** has written a different country's name on each of these racquets. He wants to start a 'League of Nations', the sign seems to say.

Why? Well, look at the floor, at the carnage of World War I, when a lack of rules meant that the game kept breaking down into devastating violence.

Sadly Woodrow gets hit on the head by a racquet, and so his founding of the League of Nations to ensure world peace, a wonderful scheme, loses its leader and goes awry.

29

At the front of the train, let's now revisit **Warren G Harding**, our warren of rabbits stuck in hardening glue to the floor of the train. They make quite a sight. They are engaged in the most astonishing range of debauched activities. Some of the rabbits are kissing, others drinking, still others playing poker. All of this activity seems to have as its focus a domed teapot too, which lies in the middle.

This may serve to remind us that Harding was a hard-drinking, gambling, womanizing disaster of a president. And that the biggest disaster of all was the Teapot Dome scandal. Look it up.

30

As we hop up the escalator our first impressions of **Calvin Coolidge** are confounded: far from looking smug, he has no facial expression at all – unsurprising, I suppose, given he's a fridge. We need a code to open up his top half, but we can guess what it is (1923) and get a look inside. All we find there, though, is a noisy radio blaring out the president's birthday broadcast on the fourth of July.

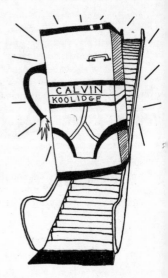

Coolidge, a president so expressionless that on being informed that he'd died one wag asked, 'How do they know?', signed the Immigration Act that, like this padlock, stopped any old Tom, Dick or Harry from getting into the US. He was also the first president to appear on the radio and the only one born on the fourth of July.

31

At the top of the escalator we find **Herbert Hoover** glumly vacuuming up the sherbet powder with a machine that he's obviously built himself. He's feeling depressed about the waste of all this sherbet, which has been prohibited.

Before becoming president, Hoover was an innovative mining engineer – a progressive who believed that there were technical solutions to all problems. He had the misfortune, though, of becoming president just before the Great Depression of 1929.

During Prohibition, by the way, he used to nip into the Belgian Embassy (which is not officially American land) to have a little drink now and again. And why not?

32

As we pass through into the first-class lounge, we can see **Franklin D Roosevelt** playing snooker – but, looking closer, we can see that he is secretly powdering the end of his cue with a Polo mint. FDR contracted polio in 1921, resulting in his complete paralysis from the waist down, a fact he kept secret throughout his presidency.

He now pots two extremely difficult balls in a row. His Japanese opponent for some reason loses his rag at this point and attacks FDR with his cue. But even after a fight on the loose-felt develops, FDR manages to pot another couple of balls; shortly after his fourth pot, he dies. Roosevelt had four successful pots at the office of President, two of them after the beginning of World War II, in which he led America.

33

Our pianist over by the bar, **Harry S Truman**, is meanwhile refusing to play anything other than a collection of what he calls 'atom-bomb ballads'. We go over to suggest a change but he says, 'It's misery, me sorry,' (sic), before explaining, 'Me very very sorry for the misery.'

Truman had dreamed of being a bar-pianist, but ended up as the only president to have come from Missouri and drop an atom bomb on civilians, or either indeed. He talks like this because he didn't go to college, a rarity for modern presidents.

34

Closer inspection of the D-shaped bar, just adjacent, reveals that it has been decorated like a beach. 'Dee White Icetower' has been planted in the sand next to a flag bearing the words 'I like Ike'.

There hasn't been a foreigner misspelling 'Ice' here; 'Ike' was **Dwight Eisenhower**'s nickname and this phrase was his highly effective campaign slogan. The D-shaped beach of a bar reminds us that Eisenhower was supreme allied commander at the D-day landings.

35

When we are called over to board our flights, we meet **John F Kennedy** surrounded by a bevy of film starlets and other beauties working as stewardesses. Let's hope this has nothing to do with JFK's atrocious lack of marital fidelity. When we hand over our ticket, we can see he is looking concernedly beyond us. We follow his eye to see that a massive Cuban missile is trying to board. A crisis if ever there was one! No wonder he's worried.

36

The Cuban Missile Crisis was one of the major events of Pulitzer Prize-winning JFK's tenure, cut short by assassination in 1963. A second look at the **Lyndon B Johnson**s arrayed in the tunnel on the ramp suggests that they aren't *all* the real thing. Rather, it seems that the real Boris Johnson has been joined by a dog, a wife and a daughter – all of whom strongly resemble him. The wife and daughter have stethoscopes round their necks, while the dog eats a massive naan bread.

LBJ's wife, daughter and dog all shared the initials LBJ. The stethoscopes on his wife and daughter remind us of his health-care provisions for young and old. The naan-eating dog reminds us of his massive escalation of US involvement in Vietnam.

37

On to the tarmac now to re-witness the ugly scene of **Richard Nixon** trying to stow someone's son in the back of someone else's golden Ford. He's sweating horribly, and his slippery fingers fumble over the boot. Fortunately, it bursts open for him as a rocket fires off from inside towards the moon, and water floods out.

Nixon was president at the time of the first moon landings, having previously lost a narrow election to JFK after sweating too much during a televised debate. His presidency was brought to a swift end by the Watergate scandal.

38

The tyres on **Gerald Ford**'s car are inflating alarmingly as we carry on, causing us to rise up off the tarmac, losing speed. They may soon burst. One can't help noticing, also, that on the side of the car runs a curious campaign slogan reading 'Don't bother voting for Ford'.

From all this we can deduce that he reached both the office of vice-president and that of president without on either occasion being elected; furthermore that there was terrible inflation during his presidency, causing recession (in speed . . .).

39

Listen in to **James E Carter** trundling along in his golf buggy: he's just tuning into his favourite radio show: his own one.

This e-cart is going faster than us again – why the hurry always?

Perhaps the Iranian with a gun shouting, 'Hi, Jack!' may be contributing.

Carter stresses that his name is Jimmy, not Jack.

'No – hijack!' says the Iranian.

Carter was the only president sworn in with his nickname, which was Jimmy; familiarity was his watchword, and he made weekly Saturday morning radio broadcasts to the nation. One of the major events of his tenure was the Iranian Hostage Crisis (which went on for 444 days from 1979 to 1981). During this ongoing crisis, see how Carter crashes his cart into the plane's steps (after also being hit by Ronald's election ray-gun).

40

Ronald Reagan, on those steps, is really acting out his role of action hero; a camera crew on the tarmac is recording it all. A line of Russians, meanwhile, is lining up, trying to force their way on board by throwing ice cubes at the president. Reagan zaps back at them liberally with his ray-gun, which warms them up nicely, thus melting their aggression and ensuring that we are first on the plane.

This all indicates that Reagan was a former actor, but also that his political persona was primarily one built around his screen presence. The warming of the Russians reminds us that it was during Reagan's presidency that the Cold War finally ended.

41

In the cockpit, **George H Bush** the elder has a golf club to hand. He's been pinging balls out of the window to defend the waiting queue of passengers down on the tarmac, who are being attacked. Bush waged the Gulf War of 1990 to help out the queue-waiters, the Kuwaitis.

42

Next to Bush is **Bill Clinton**, who is defending himself from a peach thrown through the window by a girl sitting on a passing airborne loo.

All this may remind us that Clinton was impeached for his affair with a girl on a loo-in-(the)-sky, that's Monika Lewinsky. And we shouldn't be surprised that Clinton is made of money: his tenure resulted in a huge budget surplus of $559 billion.

43

The forty-third president, the younger *Bush*, who is sitting in his father's seat, is also playing a little golf – out of the window. He has three vests on, and, like any small boy these days, he spends all his time texting when he should really be piloting the plane.

George W Bush waged war, like his father, in the Gulf. His three vests tell us that he has been arrested three times in his life, while his spending time texting reminds us of his penchant for spending a great deal of his presidential time in Texas.

Well done, you've got to the end again. Now make for a quiz and express yourself!

PRESIDENTS OF THE USA

George Washington
John Adams
Thomas Jefferson
James Madison
James Monroe
John Quincy Adams
Andrew Jackson
Martin Van Buren
William Henry Harrison
John Tyler
James K Polk
Zachary Taylor
Millard Fillmore
Franklin Pierce
James Buchanan
Abraham Lincoln
Andrew Johnson
Ulysses S Grant
Rutherford B Hayes
James A Garfield
Chester A Arthur
Grover Cleveland

Benjamin Harrison
Grover Cleveland
William McKinley
Teddy Roosevelt
William Howard Taft
Woodrow Wilson
Warren G Harding
Calvin Coolidge
Herbert Hoover
Franklin D Roosevelt
Harry S Truman
Dwight Eisenhower
John F Kennedy
Lyndon B Johnson
Richard Nixon
Gerald Ford
James E Carter
Ronald Reagan
George H Bush
Bill Clinton
George W Bush

PRIME MINISTERS OF GREAT BRITAIN

So here we are gathered together outside the front door of 10 Downing Street – fantastic that you've made it. Our tour through the prime ministers of Britain begins in just a few moments, and by the end of it you'll have learned all fifty-two of them in order. Which is pretty cool.

And what perfect timing! It's the general election today, you see. And, what's more, the polls are saying it's going to be the tightest election in history: two votes, three at most, will decide the outcome.

In other words, on top of learning all the prime ministers, between us we effectively get to add one to the list (if we can find a polling booth, that is). What a day we have in store for ourselves . . .

Whoa! Did you see that? A burglar has just come hurtling through one of the upper windows of number 10. He's not hit the ground, though. Look – he's managed to grab hold of a flagpole in the wall above the door, and he's clinging on to it for dear life.

There's a *robber* on a *wall-pole* above the door at number 10: it's Sir *Robert Walpole*, the first prime minister of Great Britain.

The way this sack-laden robber is swinging around, you have to fear for the safety of the guy standing beneath him. Look at him all unawares, running his little betting stall there on the doorstep and calling out, 'Biggest spend wins double!'

He's offering a prize, this guy, to the person who can

spend the most money. Spend the most and win double your money back. He calls it a spending competition. Everyone is getting stuck in, desperately trying to out-spend each other.

What a sensational con! And this man running the *spending competition* is *Spencer Compton*, our second PM.

Spencer Compton has not fooled everyone, though. Watch – he's being pelted with hams as we speak. Someone isn't happy!

The 'someone' in question is, in fact, a giant hen. Look at the way he flicks the hams with his wing: amazing technique!

This *hen pelting hams* is *Henry Pelham*, the next PM.

Though it would be fun to stick around and see what comes of this little conflict, we've got yet funner things to be doing with our time. Come on, follow me down here. We'll pass through the security gates at the bottom of the street and grab a boat ride from over the road – that'll get us downstream to the polling station in no time.

Approaching these gates, however, it's apparent that there's a bit of a scene going on. Outrageous! A gigantic black and white duck is on top of the gates and is making a fearful din

– perhaps he's declaiming on some vital election issue?

But no – that's a football song. And, now we're a bit closer, you can see that it's the black and white kit of Newcastle United that this song-singing duck is wearing.

This is the *Newcastle duck* on top of the gates – or, rather, the *Duke of Newcastle*, Thomas Pelham-Holles.

Ducks are **dukes**, you see, on this walk: each time you see a duck, you should know it's really a duke.

And you can apply this knowledge at once because as we pass through the gates there's a second duck standing in the middle of the road. This, as you know, must be another duke.

Extraordinary – it's spurting out a great river of cream from enormous pink udders between its legs!

The cream looks rather appetizing, and . . . mnyum . . . ohhh . . . It is! That's Devonshire cream. Wonderfully rich. You'd never expect such quality from a duck, would you?

It's obviously a *Devonshire duck*. It represents the *Duke of Devonshire*, our next prime minister.

Right, well, let's wade through this pool of cream over the road to the riverbank, where the gangplank leads down to our boat. *Squelch*, *squelch* (this certainly cools the feet, eh) and here we are.

Surprisingly, guess who we find on the gangplank, waddling down towards the boat? It's that Newcastle duck  again, the Duke of Newcastle. Hello! This must be the second term as prime minister for the Duke of Newcastle.

Hold on a second, let me just get this straight in my mind. First we had that robber on a wall-pole above the door of number 10 – that was Robert Walpole, the first prime minister. Beneath him was the chap running a spending competition. That was Spencer Compton – who was being pelted with hams by a hen, or Henry Pelham.

We passed out of Downing Street through the gates and under the Newcastle FC-supporting duck, the Duke of Newcastle. And then we had to ford the pool of cream that the Duke of Devonshire had gushed out.

Now we're seeing a bit more of the Duke of Newcastle, here on the gangplank down to our boat.

That makes for the first six PMs, with the Duke of Newcastle appearing twice.

Quickly now! The boat is about to depart. Leapfrog the waddling Newcastle duck; on to the deck we hop!

But this is most unusual. In the middle of the deck, there's a man on the loo. And it gets worse: he's got a large pot of stew by his side and he's messily flicking juicy chunks of meat on to the canvas in front of him with a brush.

The guy is doing *stew art* on the *john*. His name is *John Stuart*, and he's our next prime minister.

Now would you look at those boots dangling from his ears! Why is he wearing them?

Well, he's wearing earrings because he's an earl, and these earrings have boots on because John Stuart was the Earl of Bute.

That's the thing about **earls** on this tour: they've always got something going on with their **ears**. Sometimes, like here, it's earrings; other times, it's earmuffs. It varies. But whenever there's something ear-y happening, you can be confident in saying to yourself 'aha – we have an earl'.

But uh-oh! The Earl of Bute's artistic flicking is beginning to degenerate – some of us passengers are beginning to get hit by the odd chunk of stew.

And by God! Did you see that? A great big hunk of meat just knocked a delicate old lady over the side of the boat! No sound of a splash – all we hear is a kind of *crunch-crunch-crunch* noise, as if the old bird's landed in some gravel or something – which can't be right.

We rush to the side to see what's up – and OH NO!

IT'S JAWS! The gran is being eaten by Jaws the shark! She obviously fell straight into his mouth! He must have been waiting here for bits of stew or something . . . Oh, but this is horrible – he's wolfing her down. He's eating her whole . . .

This *Jaws* who's having a *granful* is *George Grenville*, the next prime minister.

The beast! He's going to pay for this! Come on

– after me! We'll have him if it's the last thing we do!

Pow! Take that you miserable shark, and this – *wop!*

Oops – I think I may have miscalculated here. The shark has begun to eat us too. Fight for your lives!

Thank the Lord for the emergency services; a rescue helicopter has arrived already – that's quick work. They're throwing a rope down as we speak to pluck us out of harm's way.

But what have they done this for? They've gone and attached a ham to the end of the rope – the idiots! It's rocking back and forth in the wind; it's impossible to grab hold of.

This *rocking ham* represents Rockingham, the next prime minister. As he sweeps past again, notice how he's got an S branded into his side.

Things **marked with S** on this tour are of course marquesses. This, our next prime minister, must then be the *Marquess of Rockingham* – and he's swinging past once more now. Hands at the ready!

We've got him! Right! GET US OUT OF HERE!

Someone above us does just that, and soon we're being reeled up and out of the danger zone.

You'll never believe who is hauling us in. Up above – this is incredible – is a mere boy. He looks exactly like Just William and in the squeakiest of voices he's telling us to hold on for just a few seconds longer.

But as he pulls us into the helicopter

and we catch a better look at him we spot something odd about this young Just William.

He's got scraggly grey armpit hair. And a wrinkled face. Repulsive.

This is no normal Just William: this *William* with the *elderly armpits* is *William Pitt the Elder*.

What's more, he's got piglets, miniature hams, attached to his earrings, and it's they who were chatting to us so squeakily. These *chat*tering mini-*hams* on his *ears* remind us that William Pitt the Elder is the *Earl* of *Chatham*.

Now we're safely inside the chopper, let me just explain a quick thing about Just Williams. We're going to see a fair few of them today and what you have to realize is that wherever there's a schoolboy, anyone dressed like Just William in other words, his first name will be William. Simple, really, but it does need saying: if someone's dressed as a **schoolboy**, he's a **William**.

Right – time to locate our doctor; we've picked up some pretty hefty injuries here.

Harumph. The doctor, the duck over there in the corner, is being sat on by the tennis player Steffi Graf. A (doctor) *duck* with *Graf on* – that's no doubt the *Duke of Grafton*, our next prime minister. Which is great, but he's the only doctor present and, unless she gets off him, he won't be much use to us.

We politely ask Steffi to move, but she tells us to find our own doctor. How rude! We'll have to look for other options.

Talking of which, what on earth . . . ? The pilot has just buzzed straight past a hospital . . . does he not understand we're injured? What's going on here?

The duke explains that the pilot worships the north, he

lauds it. He actually considers it blasphemy to move in any other direction. That's why he can't stop at the hospital we just passed – it would have required going a bit east.

A quick aside: people titled 'Lord' on this walk can be spotted by their religious actions or inclinations. If you notice anyone showing **religious** interest in anything, it's almost certainly because he's a **lord**.

Take our pilot, for instance, who's also our next prime minister. He worships the north – and his name's *Lord North*.

Let's see if he's ripe for conversion. I'll just tap him on the shoulder to see if there's any chance he'll at least make an exception for us shark-attack victims.

COR!

His head has just spun clean round on its axis, and we're now staring at the horrible burnt features of Freddy

Krueger. What a shock! What a way to discover that Lord North's first name is Freddy!

With nostrils flaring angrily, Freddy North tells us what the deal is. Basically, if we can get an ambulance to wait at a spot due north of here, he'll drop us off. Otherwise, forget it.

We call the ambulance service, but they say all the trained paramedics are off voting in the election. Hmm. But they could send out a team of schoolboys instead, if that's of use?

Well, it'll have to be. And, no, we don't mind if they signal their position with a flare rather than a radio. So long as it works – it had better.

This is touch-and-go stuff. If we don't find them soon, we're done for.

But LOOK! A plume of smoke! And, yes, the ambulance too, waiting on a bridge! The plan is working!

Freddy has spotted it as well, and now he's manoeuvring the helicopter towards it as we clamber back aboard our roped ham, preparing to be lowered down. With the chopper now directly over them – take a deep breath and JUMP!

Wheeee! This is cool. This is our second go on the Marquess of Rockingham, and his second term as prime minister. But without Pitt to help lower us down this time, we're stuck rocking back and forth ten yards short of the road. What do we do next?

Snap! Whoooah . . . SPLAT.

Ouch. Well, Rockingham breaking his rope like that kind of made our decision for us! And what a right old mess we're in now!

The question has to be asked: how is it that in just twenty minutes we've gone from happily getting on to a boat in the centre of town to lying dazed on a road with a shark bite and goodness knows what other injuries?

Well, after John Stuart, Earl of Bute, it was that shark, George Grenville, who put a spanner in the works by having his fill of someone's poor gran . . . and then trying to eat us too. Luckily, we'd already called in the rescue helicopter and were saved in the nick of time by the Marquess of Rockingham, that S-marked ham rocking in the wind.

It was then William Pitt the Elder who actually hauled us in on Rockingham's rope, but the only doctor on board was a duck being sat on by Steffi Graf: the Duke of Grafton. Since the pilot, Freddy 'Krueger' North, wouldn't alter his direction, we were ferried all the way out here. We tried to get down as we'd come up, on the Marquess of Rockingham

– but this second time his rope snapped, and here we are – a mess on a pavement.

On the plus side, at least we're alive – and next to an ambulance. And now one of the paramedics is approaching.

I hope he knows what he's doing; he really is only a boy, another Just William. What's more, he's on fire.
Or at least his earrings are.

He's got two great shells dangling from his earlobes, each belching out stonking quantities of green smoke.

This schoolboy smoke-signal with his *burning shell earrings* is William, *Earl* of *Shelburne*. He's our next prime minister.

And he's not bad at his job. Quick as a flash, he's heaved us into the back of the ambulance and closed the door behind us. Now he bangs twice on the back; at this signal the vehicle immediately screeches off.

We're on our way to the hospital at last – congratulations us.

Looking around inside we see what a funny old ambulance this is! It looks more like a cellar: dusty bottles of port line the walls and there's not the slightest sign of any medical equipment.

Sitting at our bedside is another schoolboy – this one with the body of a duck. He's currently busy pouring out a tankard of port.

And, before we realize what he's about to do, he slugs the whole thing down our throats.

Whewee! That puts a bit of fire in the belly, eh? And you know what – it really takes the edge off the pain too. Very nice.

This schoolboy duck-doc who believes that port is the solution to all problems, this *duck* who lives in *port-land*, so to speak, is William, *Duke* of *Portland* – our next PM.

Unfortunately, the high standards of care we've seen from the Earl of Shelburne and the Duke of Portland aren't being kept up by the third of the three schoolboy paramedics, the driver. He's doing a wretched job.

I mean – what's this all about? He is letting us sit idly in a traffic jam as he deodorizes his armpits with talcum powder. Where's the urgency in that?

If you look at those pits, you'll see they don't need powdering at all – there's not a hair in sight. Those are the armpits of a very *youthful* Just William. The boy is obviously *William Pitt the Younger* (our next prime minister), and he needs to get a move on.

'Come on, driver!' we plead. 'Sound the blooming siren! We're losing blood back here!'

At this, William Pitt the Younger seems to remember his job and, taking a long stick, leans out of the window and gives a hefty whack to the hen that's been riding along on the bonnet.

An ear-splitting NEE-NOR suddenly blasts out of the bird – this is much better than a normal siren. This is a truly toneful sound!

This *hen* who's *adding* so much *tone* is *Henry Addington*, the next prime minister. And the cars around us take notice, clearing a path so that we can speed on to the hospital.

What an adventure we've been having! Since the Marquess of Rockingham's rope snapped (during his second appearance) we've been rescued by the unlikely combination of three Just Williams and a hen. The first William was William, Earl of Shelburne – he was the one who burnt his shell earrings to help us spot the ambulance from the chopper in the first place, then heaved us into the ambulance; the second was the one inside, the duck who fed us a pain-killing pint of port – he was William, Duke of Portland. Completing the hat trick of Williams, our hygienic driver, meanwhile, was William Pitt the Younger.

Lastly, it fell to a tone-adding hen to clear us a path through the heavy traffic (that was Henry Addington).

And we're nearly there now; you can see the hospital and Accident and Emergency looming up in front of us. What a relief!

But it's looming too fast . . . for God's sake, slow down! KWANG!

What a smash-up! Dear me – we've just wrecked the front of the hospital. The driver is going to have some serious explaining to do.

And here he is, opening the back doors. But don't shout at him – he looks in a bad way, does Pitt the Younger, appearing here for the second time: his second term as prime minister. He's rather tottering from side to side, isn't he, and, whoops, he's just keeled over dead. That's the end of him, then. Disappointing: who's going to help us now? We're in no fit state to walk: shark bites and port haven't really left us with much athletic ability.

But the place is strangely deserted. The only person who might be able to help is, I'm afraid, clearly a cannibal.

I mean, just look at the young schoolboy over there on that bench. Despite the crash, he doesn't seem to have noticed we're here at all – he's too busy wolfing down his own grandma.

What a horrendous din he's making. He sounds like a dog chewing a bone. He's a very small lad, yet he's still managing to scoff down an impressive amount of her.

William *Grenville*, this boy having a *granful*, is actually the next prime minister.

We have to ask, why is he eating his gran? He's not a shark, after all – what excuse can he have?

Well, it turns out that this is a religious thing. It's his way of prayer, to eat a granny. He *lauds granfuls*. He's *Lord* (William) *Grenville*.

Golly! Was that a bottle I heard breaking? And what's this shuffling sound behind us? Oh – but of course! The duck, the Duke of Portland, who I'd completely forgotten about, is still in the back of the ambulance.

He appears to have regained consciousness, and he's coming to help us out.

He scoops us up as best he can in his duck wings, hops down on to the pavement and waddles us into A and E. Through the doors we go, and here we are at the front desk. A very useful second term as prime minister, then, from the Duke of Portland – who's now disappeared.

A man in front of us in the queue is jabbering away at the lady behind the desk about how he'll spend a whole purseful of money if she'll just sing him a song. 'A whole purseful,' he repeats. And, as he does so, he hoists a massive purse above his head and sends a deluge of golden coins sprinkling down on to the counter. This man *spending a purseful* is *Spencer Perceval*, the next prime minister. But the receptionist is having none of it. Why would she? She's Cilla Black. She knows how to say no and, besides, she stopped her singing career long ago. She pushes Spencer Perceval away and turns to us with a thrilling smile – oh, Cilla! And what lovely earrings those are – with the Liverpool FC badges rendered in silver and rubies.

Cilla is obviously a proud citizen of Liverpool. Indeed, with these earrings of hers, she's the *Earl of Liverpool* – our next prime minister.

Meanwhile, she's no longer looking very impressed. We explained how we were bitten by a shark and that we need immediate surgery – but she doesn't believe us.

'Ah can smell the drink on yeh,' she says. 'Eee, ah know yoower kind, thoow. Yer pyoower selfish. Dunna yeh know we've got noo doctors today. Thur off votin'. Goo clean yerself oop in t'toilets and stop makin' demands. Off yer goo!'

And to think how nice she seemed on *Blind Date*!

But we'll do as she says. Before that, though, I think we deserve a recap.

After the crash, Pitt the Younger let us out of the ambulance – but then died, didn't he, in the middle of his second term, leaving us stranded in the back of the ambulance. We sought help, but the only person in view, a schoolboy on a bench, was more interested in religiously eating himself a full portion of his gran: that was Lord William Grenville.

So we were rescued by the Duke of Portland, who woke up to carry us out of the ambulance and through the doors into A and E – that was his second term as prime minister. He took us as far as reception.

There, we saw Spencer Perceval spending a purseful of money on Cilla Black behind the front desk. She had nice Liverpool FC earrings but a terrible personal manner, did the Earl of Liverpool. She told us to clean up our act in the toilets. And that's not such a bad idea, come to think of it. Off we go; the toilets are just through this door.

But oh no! I'm not sure if I can cope with another one! There's a shark in here – grinning at us cunningly as he protrudes from his tin can at the urinal.

This cunning *Jaws* in a *can* is no doubt *George Canning*, the next PM. We'll steer well clear of him

and use one of these cubicles instead. Opening the first door, though, we're almost blinded by the scintillating radiance of what appears to be the Lord God Himself, sitting on the toilet.

I'm nothing if not an opportunist. So I can't help myself asking a question that's always fascinated me: 'How much money do You earn in a year, God?'

With a tremendous shrug, the god-like figure on the loo replies, 'Why count? God is rich.'

A good point. But to understand the meaning fully, we need to be clear that when people ask, 'Why count?' on this walk, what they're really trying to tell us is that they are a viscount. This person who says, '*Why Count? God is Rich,*' isn't God at all: he's *Viscount Goderich*, our next prime minister. Did you see that shrug of his? That's what people do with their shoulders when they ask why-count questions. Look out for it later.

We now edge back from his cubicle towards the two basins behind us, closing the door on Viscount Goderich.

At the left-hand basin – check this out – there's a duck with a Wellington boot stuck on his head. He's bent right under the roaring hot tap, trying to wash all the mud off.

That head-boot is getting a serious blasting: muddy water and clods of grass are being splattered all over the place – which has begun to smell of a rugby scrum.

No doubt this *duck* with the *Wellington* on is the *Duke of Wellington*, our next prime minister.

At the basin next to the duck's, meanwhile, the tap is also being put to good use. A large teapot, full of Earl Grey teabags, has stretched its spout towards the tap and is filling itself with hot water.

This pot of Earl Grey tea is, in fact, *Earl Grey* – the next prime minister.

I'll nudge Earl Grey aside, just for a second, so that we can clean ourselves up a little. Put him back in position once you're done and we'll make for the hand dryer in the corner.

Oh, how cute! There's a schoolboy lamb trying to dry himself under the machine. He's standing on a hat in an attempt to reach the button, but he still can't reach to turn the machine on.

Bless! Someone press it for him. There we go – see how much he's relishing the blast of hot air.

This *lamb* dressed like *Just William* is *William Lamb*.

Once we've dried ourselves a bit, we head straight for the exit.

But who's here blocking our way, bouncing around like a glorified pinball? It's the poor old Duke of Wellington!

He's trying to get out of the door but can't see where he's going because of that blasted boot. This is the Duke of Wellington's second term as prime minister.

We leave him to deal with his issues and pass through the door ahead of him. Let's go across to the waiting room where there appears to have been a total breakdown in behaviour . . .

Look at these two policemen playing strip catch with the schoolboy lamb. The rules seem to be the same as in strip poker: get caught out and you peel off an item of clothing.

These two *bobbies peel*ing their clothes off are identical – they're both *Bobby Peel*.

Sir Robert Peel was prime

minister either side of the second appearance of William Lamb, who's airborne, as you can see – and now wearing his Aussie hat.

One interpretation of the scene would be to call it a lamb sandwich: after Wellington's second term at the exit to the toilets the prime ministerial sequence goes Peel, Lamb, Peel.

An amusing thing to note is that the two bobbies are counting each successful catch: 'One Melbourne, two Melbourne, three Melbourne . . .' they chant.

As you'd imagine, the lamb thinks this is really stupid, even if his hat does say MELBOURNE on it. With an airborne shrug, he bleats, 'Why count Melbourne? It's a city, for goodness' sake. There's just one of them.'

A good point. But William Lamb has just let slip his aristocratic title: Viscount Melbourne.

I think we deserve a recap.

So after Cilla at reception, our Earl of Liverpool, we went into the toilets – where we were immediately freaked out by the sight of Jaws in a can at the urinal (that was George Canning). So we made for one of the cubicles to have a bit of a sit-down. Viscount Goderich was inside, though, imitating God and shrugging expansively as he asked, 'Why count? God is rich?'

At the basins, a duck was on the left-hand side washing the Wellington boot on his head – he was the Duke of Wellington; on the right, there was a pot of Earl Grey tea representing the following PM, Earl Grey.

When we went to dry ourselves we met the schoolboy lamb, William Lamb, trying to reach the dryer. It was shortly after that (at the exit) that we passed the Duke of Wellington for the second time.

In the waiting room, two bobbies, intent on playing strip catch, were peeling their clothes off as they tossed William Lamb back and forth. The bobbies peeling represented

Sir Robert Peel's two terms as prime minister, separated by Lamb. Viscount Melbourne bleated the question, 'Why count Melbourne?' in response to the policemen's pointless chanting. So Peel, Lamb, Peel were our last three prime ministers.

But listen to this good news! The surgeons are back! Off we struggle to the operating theatre.

Here it is. Let's push the door open . . .

By golly – this is more like a farmyard than a surgery. There are animals all over the place. Maybe we've made some kind of mistake.

But no. Out of this zoo, a doctor-like Jack Russell comes yapping immediately and, without any preamble, cocks his back leg and urinates copiously on our feet.

And look at the devout expression on his face as he pees away! This is dog religion for you: treating people like loos, like *johns*; this Jack *Russell* is no doubt *John Russell*, Lord John Russell, our next prime minister.

After sniffing around our injuries, he decides that we require surgery to the leg. Barking loudly, he summons the porter over to help set us up for the operation.

A racehorse with tremendous pink earmuffs trots over at once with an operating table and, once we're safely on board, drags us into position under the bright lights of the operating theatre. He's recently run the Derby, this horse, and his earmuffs tell us he's an earl. He's the *Earl of Derby*, the next prime minister.

First things first – nobody will be cutting us open without a healthy dose of pain relief! Thank goodness, then, for the large bull that's just sidled up, also wearing earmuffs. What a

colossal syringe he's got there; he's obviously the anaesthetist. He's an *Aberdeen Angus* bull in blue *earmuffs* representing the *Earl of Aberdeen*, who follows Derby as prime minister.

Mmmm . . . morphine . . . and he also gives us an Aberdeen Angus steak to clamp our teeth down on in case we need a little something extra to cope with the pain. Well done, the Earl of Aberdeen.

I think we're just about ready for surgery. That severe-looking man approaching with surgical instruments in his hands must surely be our surgeon.

'You've been in the wars, haven't you?' he says. 'But it's all OK now. You're in good hands – literally.'

'What do you mean?' we ask.

'Listen. They don't call me Palms-of-stone for nothing. My hands are incredibly hard, yet I can perform heart surgery on a newborn mouse.'

'Palms of stone? How many of them do you have?' we ask. Argh – sorry about that question; that's the morphine talking.

Our surgeon shrugs his shoulders reproachfully.

'*Why count palms of stone?* Just let them work their magic!' he enthuses.

Our surgeon is obviously *Viscount Palmerstone*, our next prime minister.

With Palmerstone at work on the operation, let's try to keep our minds off the gore by thinking through the surgical team we just met.

At the door, there was Lord John Russell, the Jack Russell who urinated on our feet, treating us as a john for religious reasons. He seemed to be in charge, giving the orders. Then along came the Earl of Derby, the racehorse in pink earmuffs, dragging an operating table behind him. He was our porter and moved us into position under the lights.

It was there that we were injected by the Earl of Aberdeen, the Aberdeen Angus bull in blue earmuffs, and finally palms-of-stone Palmerstone introduced himself: he's our brilliant surgeon.

So, after the second Peel, our prime ministers go Russell, Derby, Aberdeen, Palmerstone.

Talking of Palmerstone – what on earth is he up to? Look at this – I thought he said he was gentle! That's certainly not what it feels like from here – he's hacking away like a deranged lumberjack!

WHOOPS! He's gone and sliced Derby's bottom! He lets off an ear-splitting neigh. Quite understandably the horse is not happy!

He absolutely flies from the room, galloping down the corridor, clattering through tea-carts and doctors as he goes. We're being dragged along behind, of course.

Yeehah! This is awesome! This, the Earl of Derby's second term as prime minister, is the most fun we've had all day. Go, Derby!

But what a shame! The crafty Palmerstone has cut us off. He's somehow taken a short cut and is blocking the way in front of us. Having calmed the runaway horse, he's now insisting on completing the surgery right here, for fear that the anaesthetic will wear off.

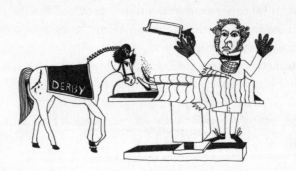

It's Palmerstone's second term as prime minister, this second bit of surgery in the corridor, and before long he announces that he's finished – before collapsing dead in a heap.

Ah! Hello to you, John Russell, our Jack Russell top doc – who's just reappeared to see how the surgery's gone. Interestingly, he's now wearing earmuffs like the other animals on the surgical team. Very stylish. He's obviously become Earl Russell in time for this, his second shot at being prime minister.

'Hmm . . . Off at the knee, eh? Perfect,' he says.

But what's he talking about? What's been cut off? What's going on here? We force ourselves to sit up so we can see what's happened.

AHHH! THEY'VE CUT OFF OUR LEG! Whoops – maybe that was a bit loud – but too late now: the horse is off again, galloping down the corridor, leaving Palmerstone and Russell, our last two prime ministers, far behind.

This is the third time Derby has moved us and his third term as PM. But whoa – there's a sharp right coming up, and we're going too fast . . .

WHAM! As Derby rounds the corner we're thrown, mattress and all, clean off the trolley and into some lift doors. At least it doesn't hurt very much – but then we're still anaesthetized.

Whewee! So, some treatment we've had, eh? Let's run through it.

We entered the operating theatre, and first of all John Russell urinated, treating us as a john, while he worked out what to do with us. Then Derby the horse dragged the surgical table into position for Aberdeen the bull to anaesthetize us before Palmerstone began the surgery.

Viscount Palmerstone was violent and careless, though, and he cut Derby (who was still tethered to the table) on the bottom. The poor horse bolted – the resultant adventure was his second term as prime minister. Eventually Palmerstone caught up with Derby, calmed him down and finished the surgery in his second term as prime minister.

During Russell's subsequent inspection of the job in his second go as prime minister, a dreadful error became apparent. When we saw our leg had been cut off, we (quite naturally) screamed our heads off. That caused Derby – this is the third time he moves us – to bolt once more. We ended up crashing off the table into these lift doors. A post-Peel summary, then: Russell, Derby, Aberdeen, Palmerstone, Derby, Palmerstone, Russell, Derby.

What adventure!

Too much adventure . . . we're getting chest pains. It's our weak heart – we're having a heart attack! Help! HELP!

Thank goodness there's someone here waiting for the lift. It's a young man wearing a baseball cap and baggy trousers. If I'm not mistaken, it's the rapper Dizzee Rascal. He certainly

looks very like him, and he talks very fast too – I can't understand a word he's saying.

Dizzee, on the other hand, clearly understands the words *we're* saying – he's preparing to give us chest compressions. Look now as he bends over and really jams his hands in over our heart, working to restart the blood-flow. Great technique:

bending to jam in his hands, *Dizzee* represents *Benjamin Disraeli*, the next prime minister.

Good effort, Dizzee. But we're still not breathing. Quick! The kiss of life!

Unfortunately, the beak of Dizzee's baseball cap stops him from reaching our mouth and he's unwilling to alter his head-gear in public, so he calls for back up.

Odd choice of back up – it's a stone. Look at him smiling down at us; what a glad stone he looks!

This *glad stone* is dressed as a schoolboy Just William but, *ewww*, he's covered in *warts*.

He now beams and leans in to give us the kiss of life, blowing stone-cold air deep into our lungs. This is the prime minister after Disraeli. He's William because he's a schoolboy, Gladstone because he's obviously a glad stone and Ewart because of those warts that make you go 'ewww'. He's *William Ewart Gladstone*.

But our heart and lungs still aren't back up and running; we're going to need another cycle of this artificial resuscitation. Dizzee now has to bend back down to jam in another set of chest compressions, followed shortly after by another of Gladstone's kisses of life.

So since we flew off the operating table and into the lift doors after our third ride with Derby (his third shot at PM) we've had Benjamin Disraeli and William Ewart Gladstone; and then Disraeli and Gladstone again, as they both had a second go at reviving us.

Bing bong.

The lift has arrived and, dear me, an enormous priest is getting out. I hope he's not here to deliver the last rites . . . But, er, no – he's brandishing a pair of defibrillators. He obviously wants to get involved in the whole resuscitation business.

With a tremendous slap to Disraeli's shoulder he cries, 'Swapsies!' and Dizzee, recognizing that he's been tagged out of the team, immediately turns on his heel and hops through the closing lift doors.

So this priest is a straight swap for Disraeli on the team, then. And a strange one. He's wearing the robes of the Bishop of Salisbury Cathedral, by the way, and there's a large S marked on the front – he's obviously the Marquess of Salisbury.

With a fruity bellow, he shouts, 'Clear!', applies the two charges to our chest and ZAP. Our whole body jolts, or at least what's left of it.

Immediately after Salisbury's zap, Gladstone comes in for another kiss of life. This is Gladstone's third go in total, his third term as prime minister.

Still, it's not quite enough. We're pretty much knocking on heaven's door here. But Salisbury is not going to give up on us.

'Clear!' he screams again as he angles in with his zappers for his second term in office. Again, we jolt like an electrified frog.

Oooooh! Was that a ripple of life we just felt in ourselves there? Keep going, guys – it's coming, it's coming . . .

Gladstone duly comes in to do his bit, this his fourth go, his fourth term as PM. Hmm, he's running out of breath; that's a bit disappointing. I think we're just about dead now. And to think all we needed was one decent shot of air!

Before we die, let's quickly relive our most recent – perhaps final – experiences.

So, since our cardiac arrest began, it's gone Disraeli, Gladstone, Disraeli, Gladstone. Then the lift arrived and Salisbury got to work with his defibrillators. The list continued: Salisbury, Gladstone, Salisbury (and one pathetic last effort from), Gladstone.

Bing bong.

The lift doors are opening. This may be the last thing we ever see.

Golly! There's a rose bush coming out of the lift . . . perhaps this is what the angel of death looks like.

The swarm of pink rose petals moves in our direction, and soon we find ourselves buried up to the ears in a rose bush.

No doubt we're being taken away to heaven.

But wait a second – I feel an arm in here, and this is a face . . . there's a man in this bush! He's giving us a beautifully rosy kiss of life. This is the stuff! I can feel my lungs kicking back into action. Who on earth could this last-minute saviour be?

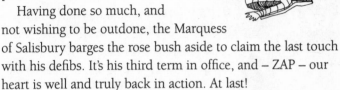

Looking closely into the roses, you can see that the bush is sprouting from his ears, which makes him, without doubt, the *Earl of Rosebery*. He's our next prime minister.

Having done so much, and not wishing to be outdone, the Marquess of Salisbury barges the rose bush aside to claim the last touch with his defibs. It's his third term in office, and – ZAP – our heart is well and truly back in action. At last!

Unfortunately, the blast of current has rather knocked us out, and we're thrown into unconsciousness. What an ordeal. Let's take stock of what's just happened.

Well, after we became detached from Derby and clattered against the lift doors, we almost died.

But Dizzee Rascal and William Ewart Gladstone tried to resuscitate us. Disraeli, Gladstone, Disraeli, Gladstone: back and forth they went with their chest compressions and kisses of life.

Then the lift doors opened, revealing the bishop-like Marquess of Salisbury with his defibrillators. Zapping-and-kissing replaced pumping-and-kissing: Salisbury, Gladstone, Salisbury, Gladstone. Gladstone's last kiss was useless, though, and it looked like we were done for.

Then, a miracle: the lift doors opened and the Earl of Rosebery, disguising himself as an angel buried in roses, came in to deliver the final kiss of life. His breath was so rosy (and unexpected) it got us breathing again.

Last of all, just to look important really, the Marquess of Salisbury applied the zappers for the third and final time, kick-starting our heart, but unfortunately knocking us out.

Tallying all this up, we've just had Disraeli, Gladstone, Disraeli, Gladstone, Salisbury, Gladstone, Salisbury, Gladstone, Rosebery, Salisbury. Nice.

But OUCH! What was that?

Coming round in what seems to be a hospital ward, some kind of cool, hard object is pinging around in the bedclothes – the last thing you want rolling around under your sheets when you've just escaped death itself. Whip back the blankets – we need to flush this thing out.

How bizarre! There's a large brown hemisphere rolling around in our bed with the number four written on it. If I'm not mistaken, that's half an outsized snooker ball, half a ball four.

This is incomprehensible . . . Ah – but perhaps it isn't. A *half a ball four* may just have been put here to remind us that *Arthur Balfour* is the next prime minister.

Looking around, we can see that there's just one other bed in the ward, directly opposite us, and a TV over to the right by the window.

We've not done very well with our fellow patients, I'm afraid to tell you. Just look at that large hen in the bed across from us, squawking away. He's waving a massive banner around in the air and shouting mindless slogans for Campbell's Chicken Soup. I think that's what they call suicidal behaviour.

This *hen* with a *banner* for *Campbell's* Chicken Soup is *Henry Campbell-Bannerman*, the next prime minister.

Forgive my lack of sympathy, but I'm just going to have to say something: 'Shut up, would you?'

Hmm. He's taking no notice. This is intolerable. Somebody turn on the TV – we'll try to drown him out.

Oh great. At the very moment we actually need the television, an ass pops up out of nowhere and perches on top of the thing as if he owns it, stopping us from turning it on.

At least he's providing some entertainment, mind – take a look at his hilarious quiff!

How's he managed it? What on earth has he put in his hair? It's shimmering with a bright white powder . . . well, there's only one way to find out. Follow me.

Whoops – I'd almost forgotten we'd lost a leg, but we can hop.

Here we are now. Hello, ass!

Come on, pat him on the head, and hold on a sec as I get a quick taster of this quiff.

Hm-mm! That's unmistakeable: it's the taste of sherbet. It's a *sherbet ass quiff*. It removes any doubt we may have harboured that *Herbert Asquith* is the next prime minister.

While you're having your go tasting that ass's sherbet, do you by any chance notice a deranged sound coming from outside?

Look! A man is trying to gnaw his way through the windows into the ward. He's frothing all over the place! How disgusting!

Could it be . . . ? Why, yes, it's Boy George! What's happened to him?

There's only one rational explanation: Boy George must have caught rabies. We're staring at a rabid Boy George. What a tragedy!

Rabid Boy George stands for *David Lloyd George*, the next prime minister.

Rabies is highly infectious – a rabid person is a health risk, regardless of their fame. Someone needs to do something about David Lloyd George here. What would happen if he broke into the ward?

Oh, but I spoke too soon: a policeman is sidling up to accost him. He's a formidable-looking officer – wielding an enormous bone in one of his gigantic hands.

This big-handed bone-carrying representative of the law is Handrew – or rather Andrew – Bonar Law.

With a single swing of the bone, he delivers a nerve-jangling wallop to the top of David Lloyd George's head, knocking him clean out.

So, since regaining consciousness, who've we seen? Well, we were woken up by that half a ball four, Arthur Balfour, who was rolling around in the bedclothes. We were then further disrupted by the hen with the Campbell-soup banner in the bed opposite: Henry Campbell-Bannerman just wouldn't stop advertising soup.

We then meant to drown out the hen with some TV, but an ass went and plonked himself on the set. He turned out to be better entertainment than we could ever have hoped for, though, once we worked out that his quiff was caked in sherbet – and that he was Herbert Asquith.

The tasty snack he afforded was interrupted, however, by rabid Boy George's slobbering at the window – David Lloyd George. And we wouldn't have dared, I don't think, risk a trip outside were it not for the handy arrival of the huge hands of the law (not to mention the bone they wielded).

All in all, come to think of it, we've got to be most grateful to Andrew Bonar Law for knocking David Lloyd George out – it means we're safe to leave this awful room.

What time is it? Did you say five o'clock? Jeez! We need to get our vote in before six. We can just about do it, I think. But we'll need to sort out our body first – we've still only got one leg.

The rehabilitation centre's just across the lawn there. Let's hop across immediately.

Boing, boing, boing. It's good to be outside, eh? The sun's shining, there's a cool breeze, patients are sporting about, healing themselves. There are even a couple of invalids just over here having something of a game of ping-pong. They've drawn quite a crowd; this must be more than your usual game. Let's have a look at how they're doing.

Hey, cool – they're on match point. I think we can spare a moment to watch this, just so long as they cut short their absurd mind games. Look at the pair of them – this is totally unnecessary. The one at the near end has taken out a Stanley knife and is shaving his head – no doubt to intimidate his

opponent. The Stanley knife makes a quite horrible grating sound as it scythes across his cranium and soon he's ferociously bald.

If this was a competition for being *bald*, this man with a *Stanley* knife would *win*. He's *Stanley Baldwin*, the next prime minister. But it's a game of ping-pong, of course, so his baldness is inconsequential.

His opponent – by golly, it's Gordon Ramsay – has an equally preposterous approach to gamesmanship.

He's staring unblinkingly over the table at Baldwin while wolfing down a Big Mac that's covered in strawberry jam. The red jam is seeping out of the corners of his mouth,

carrying flecks of burger with it. This is one of the least pleasant things I've ever seen.

Baldwin's opponent is obviously *James Ramsay MacDonald*. James for the jam, Ramsay as he's Gordon Ramsay, MacDonald for the Big Mac.

And Baldwin has served! How strange! Everything, for some unknown reason, now moves in slow motion and with every hit of the ball, another term in office passes . . .

MacDonald returns the serve into the centre of the court. Baldwin now launches an arcing topspin forehand. A stinger! Even in slow-mo that'll be hard to return.

Indeed. It takes MacDonald two touches to get the ball

back in play. But the Baldy has used the extra time to his advantage – he's walloped a pre-meditated forehand past James Ramsay MacDonald, who has no answer to the final stroke of the game.

Baldwin is the winner!

Let's replay that superb rally: after Bonar Law, the sequence of PMs went Baldwin, MacDonald, Baldwin, MacDonald, MacDonald again and, finally, Baldwin (with that last unreturned shot).

I agree with you that Ramsay MacDonald having two shots in a row (at office) seems a bit unfair, but that's exactly what he did: he changed parties, you see, so bagged two consecutive entries on our prime ministerial list.

Anyhow, though it was a lovely point on which to end the game, we've yet to vote. We'd better get back on the job.

Come on – onwards to a better body! The rehabilitation centre is just on the other side of this lawn.

And looky here, sitting outside in his impeccable naval uniform, a doorman is guarding the entrance.

And my word – he's squatting over a chamber pot with his trousers round his ankles. So what's the protocol here? Any ideas? No? Well, why don't we give him a grand salute and hope for the best.

Ha! He doesn't even notice – he is too busy navel-gazing. He just sits, trembling slightly, as he stares intently down past his navel into the chamber pot. One dreads to think what's in there!

We'd better not ask – we'll just accept that this *naval chamber*-pot man who is navel-gazing is *Neville Chamberlain*, the next prime minister.

Hop, hop, hop we go, into a gym that opens directly into a garden beyond.

The only people in this gym are, quite wonderfully, a trio of Winston Churchills. Two of them, representing our next two PMs, are huffily trying to roll an enormous orange exercise ball over towards the third – who is crouched in

wait on the far side of the room. Note how the second of the near pair of Churchills (the ones doing the rolling) looks like a caretaker – that'll help remind you that the second of Churchill's first two (consecutive) terms in office was as the head of a caretaker government (just after World War II).

Wait, though, that's not a ball the near Churchills are rolling after all: look at the thing's skin! That's clearly a citrus fruit – it must be a clementine. And, if I'm not mistaken, this clementine has a map of the world printed on to its orange surface – it's a *clementine atlas*.

It represents *Clement Attlee* – the prime minister between Churchill's second and third terms. I'm glad we cleared that up, and now we know that the sequence of PMs following Chamberlain goes: Churchill, Churchill, Attlee, Churchill (to the tune of 'Twinkle, Twinkle, Little Sta-ar').

Very good. Let's carry on into the garden, which looks very promising. It's called Medical Eden according to the sign above the gate, which also reads 'home to the tree of all therapies'.

Sweet! At our foot, a super-sized anteater sits with his long nose down a hole. He's sucking up ants and eating them with a great deal of relish – or rather *honey*.

The guy's name is An*thony* Eden, he's eatin' ants and honey in the garden of Medical Eden.

We want to ask him for guidance, but his mouth is too full of ants so we use our common sense and head straight for the tree.

Hmm. This is a worry. It has just one piece of fruit on it. A giant melon.

The strange thing about this melon is that it's dressed in full Highland tartan – kilt, sporran and all. It's even jigging around on its branch, doing the Highland fling to remove all doubt of its nationality: it's a Scottish melon. The technical term is *Mac-melon*; this fruit represents our next prime minister, whose name is *Macmillan*. Let's pluck Macmillan the magic Scottish melon from the tree and take a large bite of him. Come on.

GROW LIMBS IN A HURRY!

POW! Do you feel this powerful energy, this golden warmth, rippling through your body?

It certainly works in a *hurry*, this fruit – look! – we've grown our leg back! That really is hurried – you can't knock divine medication, eh?

This *hurried* Mac-melon also tells us that our next prime minister's full name is *Harold Macmillan*.

He's even made *us* feel hurried – which is good, because we should be. Look at the time!

We leap over the garden's back fence without delay, sprinting up the street towards the nearest taxi rank.

Bother. As we bound up to the taxi rank it's clear we're not the only ones after a car: there are a couple of others, and they're both looking pretty stressed.

Look at this first one: he's on his knees noisily licking the ground in the most ferocious manner.

'What's your problem?' we ask, a little irritably.

He says he has no problem. He's just trying to dig himself a home.

'You want to live in a hole? You want to dig it with your tongue?'

But Alec Douglas-Home is convinced that he's got *a lick* powerful enough to have *dug* himself a *home* in no time. And who are we to argue with that?

Alec Douglas-Home is the next prime minister, in any case.

The other guy has just run into the middle of the road. Look at him leaping around like a jack-in-the-box, waving his Wilson tennis racquet all over the place!

He's in a terrible hurry and he has a Wilson racquet. Let's call him *hurried Wilson* or, rather, *Harold Wilson*. He's our next PM, and he's soon telling a cabbie his destination: the polling station. Perfect – we're off to the same place.

Let's jump in alongside him.

The taxi, which is being driven by a teddy bear, is quickly on its way, and at a blistering pace.

I'm not sure this teddy driver can take the pressure of getting us there on time. As we roar down side streets and through red lights, Teddy is looking visibly uncomfortable. He is beginning to sweat. He obviously can't stand the heat.

As a teddy who can't stand the heat he represents Ted Heath, the next prime minister.

Since for safety's sake we need a driver with his wits about him, we order the teddy to pull over and, as soon as the cab has paused, our hurried co-passenger, Harold Wilson, hauls the teddy bear from the driver's seat, throwing him on to the pavement.

Hurried Harold Wilson duly hops into the driving seat himself (for his second term as prime minister), and off we speed once more towards the polling station. Gosh, this is exciting! It's right down to the wire.

Come on, Wilson! Faster! Only a hundred yards to go!

What now? What's this traffic policeman doing in the middle of the road? Look at this guy – he's some kind of gin bottle, waving at us with huge coloured hands. For goodness' sake! Not now, gin bottle!

This bottle of *gin*, his *coloured hands* now twitching at his side, is actually *Jim Callaghan*, our next prime minister. He tells us that, if we want to vote, we'll have to get there by foot. And fast – the polls will close, no matter what, in two minutes' time.

He points at a nearby thatched building. 'It's over there.'

We don't need telling twice. COME ON! To the thatched polling station!

But whoa – what's going on with this thatch?

There's a lady on a ladder with the most enormous knife in her hands, bigger than her own body. She's using it to scoop up large wads of margarine from a tub on the ground below, and she's happily slapping the yellow paste all over the thatched roof – as if it were a piece of toast.

It's very obvious who the builder is: this *margarine thatcher* has to be *Margaret Thatcher*, our next prime minister.

It looks very dangerous – but, then, on the other hand,

she does have someone to hold the bottom of the ladder for her, I notice.

It's an army *major* sitting on the *john*. It's *John Major*, a

major on the john who's making sure Maggie doesn't topple over. John Major is the next prime minister.

Why are we lingering outside, though? There's voting to be done inside!

By the polling booths, a very energetic campaigner is running around everywhere in a last-ditch attempt to make people vote for him. He's hoping to stun them with his highly unusual legs – he has no shins, and his knees, coming after the thigh in the customary manner, resemble big toes.

With these ridiculous toe-knees he nonetheless runs incredibly fast. So fast, indeed, that he's a *toe-knee blur*. This last campaigner is the next prime minister: *Tony Blair*.

With just seconds to go, we run for the booth. Who is this guy blocking our way? There's a man in brown corduroy, pulling a golden-brown cordon across the entrance. And by golly! This man with the *golden-brown cordon* has got to be *Gordon Brown*. He's trying to close up shop ahead of time! Some chance!

In one giant leap we're over the cordon, grabbing a voting slip. This is the moment we've been waiting for.

Eyes scan the list – what a glorious responsibility this is – and we select our choice for who will be the next prime minister of Great Britain!

Box ticked and paper folded, it's posted straight into the ballot box. Had we ticked an inch higher, the next four years would be different. The same goes for an inch lower. Our small action, then, has turned the fate of the nation. At least for a little while.

So that's that, then. That's the fifty-two prime ministers in all their ridiculous, tangled order. I don't want to embarrass you, but you really have done quite fabulously to get this far. Give yourself a pat on the back before joining me as we reflect on the day and see what we've learnt.

It all began with the robber on a wall-pole, didn't it, above the door to 10 Downing Street. Robert Walpole was suspended above Spencer Compton, the guy running a spending competition in front of that famous front door. He was having a rather hard time being pelted by the hen with the hams, Henry Pelham. We walked away towards the duck, or Duke, I should say, of Newcastle and passed under his gates before coming across the Duke of Devonshire, spurting cream from his udders on to the road beyond. The Duke of Newcastle appeared once more to see us down the gangplank and on to the boat.

John Stuart, Earl of Bute, was on the john doing stew art and wearing boot earrings in the middle of the deck. His careless techniques sent a gran into the Thames, and Jaws the shark soon had her in his grasp – he had his granful did George Grenville. And he would have had us too if the Marquess of Rockingham, that rocking ham, hadn't swung us up from the waters. William Pitt the Elder, the elderly Just William with the greying armpit hair, reeled us into the chopper where we soon saw that our doctor was indisposed: Steffi Graf was sitting on the Duke of Grafton.

We were quite annoyed, weren't we, by Lord Freddy 'Krueger' North's insistence that he would only go north for religious reasons, but he eventually agreed that the Marquess of Rockingham could lower us to a waiting ambulance where William, the Earl of Shelburne, was burning his shell earrings. Great smoke signals those shell earrings make. He loaded us into the ambulance where a duck fed us port – that was the Duke of Portland.

Pitt the Younger was our driver, of course, but it took the hen on the bonnet to add some tone, Henry Addington, making a siren sound before we actually got anywhere.

Pitt crashed the ambulance into the hospital, before opening the back doors for us and dying. Our hopes of surviving weren't improved when we watched as yet another William, this one a cannibal on a bench, ate most of his own grandmother: he was William 'Granful' Grenville.

The Duke of Portland finally bothered to clamber out of the ambulance and help us inside; he dumped us at reception – where Spencer Perceval was trying to spend a purseful of money on Cilla Black, the earringed citizen of Liverpool behind the desk. But the Earl of Liverpool was having none of it, and when we asked to be given favourable treatment she pointed out that there was a staff shortage and that we should probably go to the toilets to clean ourselves up.

We set off for the toilets and were soon scared out of our wits by the sight of Jaws in a can at the urinal – that was George Canning. A cubicle seemed the much safer option, and on opening the door we met Viscount Goderich who looked like God, and wouldn't count his money – 'Why count? God is rich.'

There was no space back at the basins. The Duke of Wellington, the duck washing his head-boot, took up the first basin, and Earl Grey, the pot of tea, was at the adjacent one. Beneath the hand dryer, meanwhile, we met a lamb dressed in school uniform standing on a hat: he was William Lamb.

One more sighting of the Duke of Wellington banging blindly into the door, and we were in the waiting room to watch two bobbies peeling off their clothes each time they dropped William Lamb, with whom they were playing catch. They were both the same Bobby Peel, just in different terms of being prime minister, and we discovered in the course of watching that Lamb was also called Viscount Melbourne.

Soon it was surgery time, and when we entered the surgical theatre we were rudely urinated on by a Jack Russell – we were treated as a john, by John Russell. He was the top doc, and he had the Earl of Derby bring us into position so that the Earl of Aberdeen, the bull, could inject us with morphine before Palmerstone, with his palms of stone, got stuck into some surgery.

But it all went horribly wrong.

What a fool he was, that Palmerstone, catching the horse Derby on the bottom like that with his saw! Derby bolted, Palmerstone eventually caught up to him and then Russell arrived for the post-op analysis. That was where we discovered we'd had a leg cut off and screamed so loudly that we were carried away, for the third time, by Derby – ending up being thrown against some lift doors as Derby galloped round a corner too fast.

Heart attack followed. Dizzee Rascal and that warty stone schoolboy got stuck into some chest compressions and kisses of life. Disraeli, Gladstone, Disraeli, Gladstone it went. Then the lift doors opened, and the Bishop, or rather Marquess, of Salisbury appeared and swapped himself on to Gladstone's emergency resuscitation team.

Salisbury zapped, Gladstone kissed, Salisbury zapped, Gladstone kissed. But this fourth and final kiss of life from the glad-stone schoolboy with warts was a very lame one. We were literally done for when – *bing bong* – the Earl of Rosebery, a blooming rose bush, turned up in the lift. He positively buried us in his petals, and gave us the rosiest kiss of life you could ever imagine.

That got us breathing, and after one more zap from Salisbury we were alive – if unconscious.

We woke in a ward to half a ball four, that's Arthur Balfour, spinning around in our bed. Opposite us in the ward was a hen with a banner advertising Campbell's Chicken Soup to anyone who would listen – that was Henry Campbell-Bannerman. We didn't want to listen, so went to turn on the TV but found an ass with the sherbet quiff – Herbert Asquith – sitting on it and obscuring our view.

We all had a good taste of that quiff before rabid Boy George started frothing at the window in his depiction of David Lloyd George. And it was lucky that Andrew Bonar Law, the policeman with a bone in his large hand, whacked Boy George on the head – it left the coast clear for us.

On our way across to the rehabilitation centre, we paused briefly to watch a game of ping-pong. We arrived at match point to see some gamesmanship, as Stanley Baldwin took a Stanley knife across his scalp to shave parts of his head bald, and Gordon Ramsay ate a Big Mac doused in jam – he was James Ramsay Macdonald. They had that preposterous rally that went Baldwin, MacDonald, Baldwin, MacDonald, MacDonald, Baldwin.

Sooooo silly. We hastened to the centre. At the door, our salute wasn't returned by Neville Chamberlain, who, despite his naval uniform, was too busy navel-gazing on his chamber-pot to notice us. Inside, though, we were delighted to see Churchill, Churchill again, Clement Atlee and Churchill for the last time – Atlee was the clementine atlas.

Finally we discovered the answers to our one-legged prayers. We found the amazing Medical Eden gardens where we encountered an anteater eatin' ants and honey – he was Anthony Eden. Beyond him, a tree at the back of the garden held a glorious Scottish melon that cured us in a hurry – that was the hurried Mac-melon, or Harold Macmillan.

Completely healed and in a desperate rush, we sprinted for a taxi. Alec Douglas-Home was at the taxi rank, digging himself a home one lick at a time. Fortunately, we didn't have to wait behind him and jumped into a cab with the hurried Harold Wilson, who'd waved down a ride with his Wilson tennis racquet.

The taxi driver was Ted Heath, a Teddy who couldn't take the heat, as it turned out, so he was thrown out by Wilson who took over the driving in his second stint as prime minister. We looked sure to make the polling station when a gin-bottle traffic policeman stopped us with his coloured hands. He was Jim Callaghan and he pointed us to the thatched building just yards away.

Margaret Thatcher was busily adding margarine to the thatch of this building from her ladder, which we thought quite dangerous until we noticed John Major, a major on the john, securing the base for her.

Inside the polling station, Tony Blair was charging around in a blur of his horrible toe-knees. We rushed straight for the booth, desperate to get our vote in on time, only to find Gordon Brown, our corduroy-suited PM, wretchedly attempting to keep us from voting with a golden-brown cordon. He wasn't going to stop us – we leapt right over him, and the rest, as they say, is the future.

ROUND TWO: SPOTTING THE DETAIL

After your heroic efforts in learning all of the prime ministers in order (well done, by the way), it's very possible that someone may try to persuade you that your brain has been filled to bursting point with these many facts, that it is somehow full.

You must be careful to extract the five pounds you've won off them for successfully reciting the PMs, before you explain just how wrong they are.

Memories, you can clarify, always grow out of other memories. The greater the stock of memories you have, the more opportunity there is for new memories to take root.

By learning the list of PMs, you've basically created a great deal of space in which new memories can grow – a fertile flowerbed, if you like, in which you can help cultivate a colourful garden of recollections.

What follows is a first step down that road – and a guide to the techniques involved in gardening the world of your memory. As ever, try to make sure you vividly imagine the images that follow.

1

So, here we are watching **Walpole** again, our robber leaping out of the window on to his wall-pole. And don't think it unfair that he's a crook in our story – before becoming prime minister Walpole spent time in prison for accepting illegal payments and, as all this money tumbling from his sack attests, he wasn't shy of getting his way with the odd bribe once he took office.

Look what else is spewing from his sack – that's a glass jar and, if I'm not mistaken, there's a severed ear jinkin' around inside! It belonged to one Captain Jenkins, and Walpole waged the War of Jenkins' Ear from 1739 against the Spanish for cutting it off. The whole Spanish empire in South America was briefly imperilled, but the British fought pathetically, and as a result Walpole's popularity soon declined.

2

Beneath Walpole, we've got **Spencer Compton** running his spending competition.

What an incredibly swollen ear he's got; it looks as if it's shortly going to burst with infection. These days we'd probably say that it '*will ming tons*'. This reminds us that Compton was *Earl of Wilmington*, poor man.

But what high spirits everyone in the spending competition seems to be in!

Not for long – Compton's most significant act as prime minister was to raise the duty on spirits to curb such public exuberance. This of course made him extremely unpopular, and there was huge relief when, after a short time, he died. Imagine the crowd cheering as he is brained by one of Pelham's hams (which didn't actually happen) to help you remember that he was the first prime minister to die in office.

3

And he's not the only one to be attacked by **Henry Pelham**'s pelted hams. Prince Charles is trying to get past by riding the dog Bonnie – but a single ham takes care of Bonnie Prince Charlie's little rebellion of 1745–6.

Watch now as a newly married couple tries to sneak past. The beautiful seventeen-year-old bride and her fifty-three-year-old naval-officer hubbie try to protect themselves with a giant cardboard calendar, but they can't stop the reorganization of the Royal Navy, the marriage act of 1753 (which stopped people under twenty-one marrying without parental permission) nor indeed the introduction of the Gregorian calendar (which is used to this day).

4

As we pass to the bottom of the street, you'll see that the Newcastle duck has seven buckets of water atop his gate, which he's tipping, one by one, on some beret-wearing American Indians who are trying to pass through.

Why? Well, in his first term, the **Duke of Newcastle** precipitated the Seven Years' War – a massive global conflict in which more than a million people died. You can see the beginning date (1756) on the gates. Britain fought mainly (and unsuccessfully) in the North America portion of this war, called the French and Indian War because of the opponents' nationality. The lack of success severely dented Newcastle's popularity.

5

Beyond the gates, you can see the **Duke of Devonshire** wearing a sash saying 'Mr London 1756'. No wonder – he was thought to be London's best-looking man when he became prime minister.

And now we can see why he is gushing quite so much cream; he's being milked! Look, it's that schoolboy with grey armpit hair – William Pitt the Elder. He's working the teats like crazy.

William Pitt the Elder dominated mid-eighteenth-century politics long before he actually became prime minister. He was already the dominant power within the government; Devonshire was just the pretty face of this administration.

The duck is not enjoying it at all, though, and once he's been relieved of 225 litres of cream he gives up after just 225 days in power.

On the gangplank, the **Duke of Newcastle** is standing nervously next to Pitt (again!), fretfully blowing bubbles in his bubblegum. The elderly schoolboy sets up an architect's table on the gangplank so he can design the British Empire. He's got this idea that war should be waged for trade, and he's colouring in Canada, India, West Africa and the West Indies. During Newcastle's second term, Pitt thus invents the imperial policy that will build the British Empire. The duke's bubble-blowing reminds us how his nickname was Hubble-bubble (for his hurrying everywhere and fussing so much).

166

6

Down the gangplank, past Newcastle (and Pitt) on to the boat, we can see that **John Stuart**'s john (which has a Scottish flag on it) is surrounded by exotic plants – the Earl of Bute adored foreign flora and helped found the Royal Botanic Gardens of Kew in London.

His Scottish stew art isn't very popular with us the passengers, though, and he is being roundly abused from all sides – rather like he was when prime minister.

And, given his role in the gran's death, you will appreciate that Bute died when he fell off a cliff.

7

In the waters below, while the shark **George Grenville** is digesting his granful, note how his fin has a giant stamp tacked to it. This is the harsh stamp tax he introduced to the colonies in an attempt to gain popularity by lowering British taxes correspondingly. Its introduction led to the tragedy that was the American Revolution.

8

Ah yes, here comes our rescue helicopter, just in time. As we're hoisted from the waters, note how the big S stamped on to the **Marquess of Rockingham** is peeling off. Rockingham repealed the American Stamp Act. But in doing so he peels himself out of a job, with George III sacking him for being weak-headed.

9

Like so many schoolboys, **William Pitt the Elder**, hauling us in, has a cricket bat under his arm (he was the first prime minister to show an interest in the game). He keeps shouting, 'I'm mad that I got out,' over and over again. In fact, he has gone mad and has gout. They plagued his premiership and disastrously impeded his capacity to deal with the American colonies in the run up to their Declaration of Independence.

10

Just take a closer look at Steffi Graf on her duck inside the chopper. What a youthful hairdo she has! See how her plaits each make the shape of a three in the air. The **Duke of Grafton** was just thirty-three when he became prime minister – for about a year.

You'll also notice that the inside of the chopper is full of prams and hunting equipment. Grafton had sixteen children; he was also in the habit of missing important governmental appointments to indulge his love of hunting. He didn't last long in the job.

11

Up in the cockpit our pilot, Freddie 'Krueger' North carries us twelve miles – mirroring North's twelve years as prime minister.

But the journey is a disaster. Look how *Sarah* Jessica Parker, wearing a *toga*, is fighting **Lord North** for control of the chopper. She wants to go to 'York Town' (as she calls it).

This reminds us of the battles of Saratoga and Yorktown in the American War of Independence – disastrous losses against the soon-to-be USA in a war Britain had no business losing.

Did you know that cats hate gin? The bottle of gin in North's hand is anti-cat-lick Gordon's stuff. This reminds us of the anti-Catholic unrest known as the Gordon Riots, which hastened the end to his premiership.

12

As we descend on our second **Rockingham**, the ham rocks so wildly it makes the shape of a shamrock (the symbol of Ireland) in the air. That'll be because Rockingham was a champion for Irish independence. And the rope's inconvenient snapping reminds us that Rockingham died in office – in the year 1782.

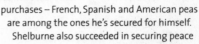

Lying dazed from our fall, we have to ask how this Just William before us manages to get his shell earrings to burn so fulsomely. The answer is that he is filling them with rice. Look he can *fit more rice* into those things than you'd ever believe. His full name is William *Fitzmaurice*, **Earl of Shelburne**.

He's been buying peas, you can see, from a little market stall on the bridge. And he has made a very international set of purchases – French, Spanish and American peas are among the ones he's secured for himself. Shelburne also succeeded in securing peace with the French, Spanish and Americans in his short term in office.

13

At last, we're off to hospital. In the back of the ambulance, among the port bottles, notice how we've been joined by more than just a schoolboy duck: it's the **Duke of Portland**.

Freddie 'Krueger' North has joined us, glowering from his seat on a curly-haired Fox.

To have curls means that you are a Charles in our story – so North must be sitting on Charles Fox, the influential MP.

Fox and North are the Fox–North coalition of 1783; it is they who are really running the country – Portland is just the titular head.

They're spending their time trying to eat a spicy Indian meal but – oh dear – it's obviously too hot for them. That they try (and fail) to eat Indian cuisine reminds us of the East India Company, which they tried (and failed) to nationalize.

14+15

Pitt meanwhile has done better – he's finished half of his Indian meal: not bad for a toddler of just twenty-four months of age. **Pitt the Younger** was twenty-four when he became prime minister (having already turned down the job three times – an amazing fact) and soon established the government as dual controllers of the East India Company.

On the subject of food, Pitt is also throwing rotten burgers out of the window as he attempts to correct 'rotten boroughs' – electoral seats which could be bought.

And see those tacks he's firing out of the window with the burgers? The wind is blowing them back in! They're incoming tacks, and remind us how Pitt introduced the first income tax, raising funds in response to the threat of Napoleon's expected invasion.

Our hen adding tone (to the siren) on the bonnet is of course **Henry Addington**. He is using a stethoscope as a microphone and is making himself comfortable, leaning back against the *middle of the glass* windscreen. Our man adding tone was a doctor before he became prime minister, and was our first *middle-class* prime minister. Occasionally, he grins at the driver William Pitt the Younger, a childhood friend of his.

When **Pitt the Younger** opens the doors of the ambulance during his second term as prime minister to let us out he unfortunately decides he'll have a quick swig of port – but he's too young for the stuff and this sip, which amounts to excessive consumption of port, is what causes him to die.

16

Over on the bench, **William Grenville** is still eating his gran. Though this is morally reprehensible and he doesn't lift a finger to help us either, he was, on balance, a very good man. Look at all these slaves running around whooping: it was Grenville who abolished the slave trade in 1807.

170

Portland, summoned again from the ambulance, struggles to carry us through the doors into the hospital: knocking into walls as his legs go wobbly with the strain. Portland's second term as prime minister was blighted by terrible ill-health.

17+18

At the front desk the tiny **Spencer Perceval** is offering the purse strings to anyone and everyone who passes. Since nobody is interested, he decides to spend the money himself – by getting up on the tips of his toes and pouring it out over Cilla's desk.

Similarly, Perceval, the shortest prime minister in history, was such an unpopular leader that despite offering the position of chancellor to at least six people no one would take it – so he did it himself.

But oh dear! A die-hard Cilla fan (perhaps) has just shot him in the head! He's been assassinated! His brains are all over the money! In 1814, Perceval, a lawyer, became the only prime minister to be assassinated.

Behind the hospital reception desk, there's the **Earl of Liverpool** – Cilla Black. She is surrounded by a field full of Wellington boots – these represent the Duke of Wellington's victories on the continent against Napoleonic forces during Cilla's premiership, victories that greatly increased the Earl of Liverpool's popularity – helping him to fourteen consecutive seasons at number 10.

Also on the desk is an angry-looking policeman with a corn on the cob for a truncheon. This corn-wielding man of the law is the 1815 Corn Law, a tax on foreign crops that Liverpool introduced to protect British farmers. But why is the policeman so angry? That's because Cilla has been *robbin' banks* when her work at the hospital *check-in is on*. The Earl of Liverpool's full name is *Robert Banks Jenkinson*.

19

Passing into the toilets, we meet **George Canning**. Or is it? Lo! That's not a real shark! That's a person in a shark-suit, surely? Indeed it is: George Canning was known for playing practical jokes.

Interesting that he was also the first prime minister to campaign widely for election: but this slogan he has up above him – Spain and Portugal – is surely a joke too?

Maybe, but look what's happening now! He's slipping into his can. We're losing sight of him! The last we see are the words 'Spain and Portugal'. These were indeed 'the lost prime minister's' last words. He was a particularly gifted man, much missed after dying in office after only a few months.

20

Viscount Goderich in the cubicle, despite the celestial light, achieved nothing of note during his premiership. As we close the door, though, he roars with delight. He was delighted to retire from office, and was much happier afterwards.

21+22

Time to wash our hands, and at the sink you'll notice that the **Duke of Wellington** has erected a protective iron cage around himself. He famously put iron shutters at the windows of his house when, because of his unpopularity, pedestrians started throwing stuff through them. That's what earned him the title 'the Iron Duke' – his iron-will and military discipline had nothing to do with the nick-name, oddly enough.

Note how there's a cat licking appreciatively in the muddy water at the basin – and no wonder: Wellington oversaw Catholic emancipation in 1829, granting almost full civil rights to them. The boot on his head, by the way, is named after him. We cast our attention next to the pot of Earl Grey tea in the adjacent basin (this variety of tea, coincidentally, was named after the same **Earl Grey** that it represents), and the seventeen miniature cups around it. With seventeen children Earl Grey holds the record for having had the most of any prime minister.

And, wow, look at this – his body is taking on a new shape … It's reforming and now looks like something between a teapot and a ballot box. This reminds us of Earl Grey's 1832 Reform Act, in which many more people got the vote, setting in motion 130 years of parliamentary reform that resulted in everyone being able to vote today (except our under-18s!).

23

Over now to the hand dryer and the adorably cute **William Lamb**.

Queen Victoria, you'll notice, is combing his hair with a biro. He was her tutor, then mentor, then close friend. That she's using a biro unfortunately reminds us of how William Lamb's wife had an affair with the poet Biro, I mean Byron, and then wrote a book about it – causing hair-curling embarrassment.

On our way out of the toilets, we ask **Wellington**, who is bumping against the door, what, exactly, he's looking for. He says he's looking for Sir Robert Peel who has been appointed prime minister, but can't be found anywhere. Wellington's second term was as a stop-gap while everyone else looked for Peel – who was off in Italy.

24

Peel, our policeman peeling his clothes off, was in fact the founder of the modern police force. Policemen are called bobbies after Bobby Peel. He's being cheered along by lots of sooty women and children as he plays catch – and quite right too: it was Peel's laws that stopped them working in the mines.

And we now understand why William Lamb, clearly a Brit, was wearing the Aussie hat with 'Melbourne' on the rim. It turns out that the Australian city of Melbourne was named after Viscount Melbourne.

The second peeling bobby now catching the lamb has got the same corn truncheon as the bobby we saw on Cilla's desk. But he is peeling the leaves off this corn very carefully – reminding us of how **Sir Robert Peel** repealed the Corn Law in his second term (1846).

25

Off we go to revisit our surgery. As we barge our way into the theatre and the Jack Russell begins peeing on our leg, notice just how weak its urine is: as clear as water. Mind you, it's no weaker than **Lord John Russell**'s wretched leadership. Which is a shame, because Russell was an imaginative and instinctive reformer who limited women's working hours and improved teachers' pay.

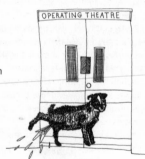

26-28

The Earl of Derby, our racehorse, has a shelf on his saddle full of *Who's Who*s, that directory of important names. Derby's cabinet was nicknamed the 'Who? Who? cabinet' after he was forced (because of infighting among the big guns) to appoint a selection of people no one had ever heard of before. The shelf also holds a copy of the *Iliad* – a poem the scholarly Derby translated into blank verse.

Next in this farmyard of an operating theatre is the **Earl of Aberdeen**. He is mooing enthusiastically, trying to gather the surgeons in a tight medical coalition. But his moo is too weak – he doesn't have the presence to control such big personalities.

The Earl of Aberdeen's coalition – featuring Russell, Palmerstone and Gladstone among others – was too big on talent and ambition to be effective, and Aberdeen was soon ousted by his eager underlings.

His appearance can't have helped – check out the *grimy criminal* look he's got going on. Aberdeen's Crimean War, a disaster of a conflict, made him very unpopular at home.

We all wondered earlier at the exceptional stillness of **Palmerstone**'s hands. It's partly down to his experience – he'd spent four decades as a politician by the time he became prime minister in 1855 at the age of seventy-one. His nickname is *Pumice Stone* – that's what his stone palms are made of – and it gives a clue as to his abrasive style.

You see that china opium pipe he's smoking that's shaped like King Kong? This should remind us of the Second Opium War in China while he was in office that won Britain the imperial possession of Hong Kong.

Palmerstone's first term ends up with him cutting a chunk from Derby's bottom. As Derby bolts and we zoom along behind him during this, the earl's second term, we manage to pilfer a whole Indian takeaway off an upended trolley – worth £18.58! This reminds us of the India Act of 1858, where the East India Company was entirely transferred to government control.

When Palmerstone rather impressively cuts us off at the end of Derby's second term, we spot some evidence of his racy private life poking from his pocket – that's a court ruling saying he's been cited in a divorce case, even though he's in his late seventies now.

He dies at the end of our surgery at the age of eighty-one, a splendid age for a prime minister.

John Russell takes over for his second term, during which he tried to liberalize trade laws. He's not really concentrating on us – he's reading a letter from his grandson, the philosopher Bertrand Russell, whom he brought up.

When we crash off the operating table into the lift doors during **Derby**'s third term as prime minister we get to see his feet for the first time: he hasn't got hooves, but rather twenty-two exceedingly expensive *toe-rings*.

This reminds us of how he was head of the *Tory* party for twenty-two years – and was in fact the founder of the party in its recognizable modern form.

Well, after landing on the floor at Derby's sudden stop, we're well into our heart attack now.

29

Dizzee **Benjamin Disraeli** is the first to start chest compressions, placing a book over our heart and pumping away with one hand. He's using the other to force bonbons into his vigorously chewing mouth.

The book is one of his witty and underrated novels, *Vivien Grey*, I believe. And he's obviously got *bonbon fever* – he's a *bon viveur*, and he feels so much like *chew*ing because he's the first *Jew*ish prime minister.

We hardly need comment on the rivalry that exists between Gladstone and Disraeli – look how they're fighting over the chance to bring us back to life.

30

Gladstone is made of stone for a very practical reason: he's a firebrand, you see, and needs the high melting point to be able to heat up like he does in parliamentary debates.

He comes back and forth so many times during our resuscitation that you have to ask where he goes when not in office. The answer is that our stone man has a heart of gold – he's nipping over to some prostitutes round the corner to persuade them to mend their ways, just as he did around London, even when prime minister; unprecedented behaviour for a PM, but very liberal.

Which should come as no surprise: he was the father of the Liberal Party.

31

Ah, the lift! Out comes the **Marquess of Salisbury** to swap places with Disraeli and work on our heart. Take a closer look this time at the S marked on Salisbury's frock.

We can see a map of Zimbabwe on his chest, and also that it is the capital of this country that's been marked with an S. S for Salisbury – it was during his time in power that Britain gained Zimbabwe (then known as Rhodesia) as an imperial colony, and its capital was named after him.

During the Salisbury–Gladstone–Salisbury–Gladstone spell, each has his own distinctive behaviour.

Gladstone, on the one hand, has begun to blow great big green bubbles in his *gum* – he's become known as the *G.O.M.*, or Grand Old Man, and now spends much of his energy trying to pass bills for Irish Home Rule. That's why the gum blows out like a shamrock completely independently of its blower's behaviour. Salisbury, meanwhile, insists on explaining everything he's doing – and making us colour in maps of the heart. It was his Elementary Education Act of 1891 that mandated free primary school education for everyone.

Don't forget the sequence of zaps to breaths: it goes Gladstone, Disraeli, Gladstone, Salisbury, Gladstone, Salisbury, Gladstone. By that last breath of Gladstone he's had four puffs, or turns in office, when …

32

Out of the lift emerges the **Earl of Rosebery**, buried in the bushes of roses sprouting from his ears. He's appeared at the last possible moment, but manages to save us for the simple reason that he's the luckiest man in Britain. Anything he tries to do comes off.

As a student, Rosebery made a list of his three aims in life: to marry the richest woman in England, to win the Derby and to become prime minister. He achieved all three. And he had little interest in clinging to the job of prime minister once he'd ticked it off his things-to-do list, which you can see him doing now.

As **Salisbury** comes in for his third and final zap, he's really become quite *bored* of the task – so bored, in fact, that he's yawning. This reminds us that the *Boer* War was taking place at this time.

33

After that last zap, we only regained consciousness when we felt half a ball four bouncing around in our bed in the ward. That was **Arthur Balfour**, and I, for one, seriously doubted whether he was real.

How apt! Balfour first became famous for producing dense works of philosophy, such as *A Defence of Philosophical Doubt* in which he argued that doubting the reality of things is, well, good practice.

And we have to doubt things rather a lot when Balfour is driving a car around our bed loudly declaring how he's working out where he'll put a new country called Israel on the world map.

As well as being a doubting philosopher, Balfour was the first prime minister to own a car. He authored the Balfour Declaration – an early step on the road to the creation of the state of Israel in Palestine.

34

Rather amazingly, **Sir Henry Campbell-Bannerman**, the mad hen advertising Campbell's Chicken Soup opposite us, is drinking Pimms. He's celebrating becoming the first PM to be called prime minister officially (there'd been various names before that, none of them as pithy). You'll notice how his cluck is distinctively Scottish – he's from Glasgow, is old Campbell-Bannerman.

And check out the bright little *jet* plane, piloted by a determined-looking woman, which he's having to *suffer* buzzing around his head: this was the era of *suffragettes* – women campaigning for the vote. Let's follow this little jet as it flies all the way over to the ass on the TV – chased by the hen's raw Glaswegian cluck.

35

It's no surprise that **Herbert Asquith**, our ass with a sherbet-encrusted quiff, is sitting with his legs over the screen on the TV. He thinks the audio is enough – and he was the first prime minister to use commercial recordings to direct public opinion via the radio.

Meanwhile, a gaggle of newly uniformed young soldiers is waiting behind us in the queue, hoping to taste glory. Asquith signs them up for the trenches of WWI, since they're here. He was the prime minister who led Britain into the Great War.

36+37

I'm not sure if this is just the rabies talking or shell shock, but rabid Boy George, beyond Asquith, has drooled a picture of a Welsh dragon stuck in barbed wire on to the window.

The only Welsh prime minister to date, **David Lloyd George** led Britain for the second half of the nightmare of WWI and is remembered as the Man Who Won the War.

And hello again to **Andrew Bonar Law**, our bone-wielding law enforcer, who was born in Canada. You can tell from the flag he's got on the top of his hat. He must have attempted to knock him out – now he's carrying Lloyd George away.

Well, of course! Bonar Law was in coalition with Lloyd George – though he did break from it in due course to become PM. As an aside, he once said the following: 'If I am a great man, then a good many great men of history are frauds.'

38

Let's head out of the ward again. Over at the ping-pong table, **Stanley Baldwin** wants to win so badly because lots of people have come to see him. He feels it would be 'social justice' if he, the crowd's favourite, won. As a politician, his actions were dominated by such concern for social justice.

He's just paused for a bite of Mr Kipling's cakes to gain some energy before this important match point – well, he *was* Rudyard Kipling's cousin.

39

Ramsay MacDonald, for his part, is eating a Big Mac – but he's also giving birth. A noisy process that reminds us of how he was the first Labour prime minister.

He's about to give birth to a shower of little James Bonds, who will all tumble on to a soft field of margarine below. This margarine field of Bonds reminds us that Ramsay was the first PM to include a woman, Margaret Bondfield, in his cabinet.

So, the rally starts: Baldwin to MacDonald, back to Baldwin, back to MacDonald who then takes out a paddle with the Union Jack on it for a third strike. This was where he became the leader of the National Labour Party, as opposed to the normal one. National or not, he fails to return Baldwin's third strike as PM.

40

Poor **Neville Chamberlain** is up next. His chamber pot is full of really expensive German peas – Chamberlain having sought peace with Germany at any price. The trouble is that he was sold the peas by a man named Hitler – and they're fake. That's why he's too upset to acknowledge us as we walk past – history does not smile upon his policy of appeasement, rather unfairly, and he is often thought to be personally responsible for WWII.

41+42

Here we are now with our Churchill–Churchill–Attlee–Churchill jamboree. The first **Churchill** is carrying a hat stand covered in party gear – a memento from his birth in a cloakroom during a dance at Blenheim Palace. But you probably already know more about Churchill (great saviour of Britain, of the free world indeed, during World War II) than could be fitted in this book, so we'll carry straight on past. **Clement Attlee,** our clementine atlas in the middle, is being polished by nurses – and he deserves it: he founded the NHS. He also has an ATM in his side with a Union Jack showing on the screen – which reminds us that he nationalized the Bank of England.

You may wonder how a fruit became arguably the most successful prime minister of the twentieth century, but he pipes up now to offer us an explanation: 'Often the experts make the worst possible ministers in their own fields. In this country we prefer rule by amateurs.'

Our third Winston Churchill is shivering dreadfully on the far side, and looking terribly aged. As the clementine reaches him, his hands are too cold, his legs too tired, to do anything with it. This is a clue to Churchill's third term as prime minister, a frustrating spectacle as the great man found himself at his very advanced age quite unable to resolve the Cold War as he had hoped.

43

Anthony Eden, our anteater who's
eatin', has his long nose down a hole;
he's snuffling around for food. Note the
trademark homburg hat (often now
called an Eden, after this prime minister)
and the way he's using his military cross,
won for bravery in WWI, as a plunger to
test the depth of this ant colony.

But, dear me, he's just realized that
this is a sewer and not an ant colony that
he has his long nose down! Yuk! Eden's career was ruined by the Suez crisis,
in which he schemed and lied enough to justify this long nose of his.

44

In need of healing in a hurry, we head towards
the tree-of-all-therapies, where **Harold Macmillan**
the Scotch melon greets us amiably. He seems to
be really enjoying defrosting in the sun; indeed,
a warming in Cold War relations, combined with
gains in Britain's prosperity, meant Macmillan
enjoyed a hugely successful first term. And, yes,
that is a Supermac badge he's got on his belt.
Supermac was what we Brits used to call him.

Unfortunately, when we move close to him, he
becomes a bit uncomfortable at the scandalous
amount of perfume we're wearing and starts
blustering, just like his inept response to the
Profumo scandal that marred his latter days as
prime minister.

45

Along at the taxi rank, **Alec Douglas-Home** is
licking himself a hole so he can make a nice
secret home for all his aristocratic regalia. He
had to put away his aristocratic title to join
the Commons after becoming prime minister.

You'll notice he's also burying his cricket
bat: a keen sportsman in his youth, he
remains the only prime minister to have
played first-class cricket.

Our hurried tennis player, in between
waving for a cab, turns to abuse Alec Douglas-
Home every so often for being quite so aristocratic. Just as he did,
mercilessly, in the Commons.

46

Generally speaking, however, **Harold Wilson** has a rather intellectual look to him. And when we get into the cab he insists on putting on an Open University tape about the ethics of capital punishment. This relates to two of Wilson's momentous achievements: he oversaw the foundation of the Open University and also the banning of capital punishment.

Once in the cab, I have to confess that I'm finding all this speeding very frightening – and I can't help myself embracing Wilson, hugging him close to reassure myself. He doesn't mind in the least, of course, even if my gesture had been romantic: it was he who legalized expressions of physical affection between men in 1967.

47

Wow – look at our cab driver's body! The more pressure we put on this teddy to get a move on, the more sawdust begins to fly from its seams. But this shouldn't surprise us: **Edward Heath** was, after all, the son of a carpenter.

He's done something very clever here, though, has Teddy Heath: he's installed a European flag on the bonnet, which makes everyone think we're a diplomatic vehicle and they make way for us.

So too did Heath enter Britain into the European Community without anyone managing to object too much.

But his slowness prompts a show of hands on whether the ted should continue. Although he receives more votes than **Wilson**, who wants to replace him, Wilson still

kicks him out of the car. In the general election of 1974, Ted won more votes than his opponent, but found himself out of a job regardless.

With Wilson driving the car, we zoom along until we reach the traffic policeman with the coloured hands waving us down in the road.

48

This man is the tallest person we've seen all day – six foot one – a towering height for the late seventies. **Jim Callaghan** has got a big sunny smile on his face despite the (extremely local) blizzard that's coating him in icicles.

He managed to live up to his nickname, Sunny Jim, during the Winter of Discontent in 1978 (when industrial action brought the nation to a standstill). During the crisis, he was photographed laughing away on a foreign beach as the nation saw rats infest the streets and unemployment rise to historic highs. He wasn't very popular as a result, and was soon booted out of office.

49

At last, the end is in sight as we head once more towards **Maggie Thatcher**'s thatching operation. The first thing to note is that her iron ladder has eleven rungs, which reminds us that Maggie, the 'Iron Lady', was prime minister for eleven years. She is using her margarine to seal holes in the roof. From these holes, you can see miners fleeing: **Thatcher** controversially closed most of the nation's coal mines.

And now look: an Argentinian footballer is bounding across the roof to attack Maggie with a fork – but she squashes him brutally into the thatch with her knife. It was of course Margaret Thatcher who responded so decisively to quash the Argentinians during the Fork-lands, or rather Falklands, War.

50

At the bottom of the ladder, **John Major** has a very well-decorated army major's uniform. First, he's got a miniature Volkswagen Golf on his shoulder – representing the first Gulf War.

He's also got an Irish flag on his breast, made entirely from peas, a symbol of the peace in Northern Ireland, which he all but secured. Finally, imagine he's wearing an 'I love Brixton' badge from his time growing up in South London.

It's also worth pointing out his enormous clown shoes, which belonged to his father. Major remains the only prime minister whose father worked as a clown.

51

Inside the polling station, here's **Tony Blair** with his toe-knees blurred, running around doing his last minute campaigning. To be sure, he's very young (the youngest prime minister since the Earl of Liverpool – back at the hospital's front desk) so you can expect a certain amount of vigour. But what exactly is he up to?

Well, Tony is running so much because he likes to do everything and be everywhere: as prime minister he assumed almost presidential control of all aspects of government. But right now he's trying to grab some stuff off a high rack. He can't reach, though, because he has no shins.

In his desperation to get to the stuff on the *high rack* he puts in huge amounts of effort: his maimed legs go into overdrive and spin a million times in just a couple of minutes. This all reminds us of the political spin that accompanied Blair's attempt to conquer *Iraq*, and the disaster it turned out to be when more than a million Iraqi people were killed or seriously hurt.

52

With seconds to go, here's **Gordon Brown** again, pulling his golden-brown cordon across the voting booth. He's trying to cancel the election. When Brown became prime minister after Blair resigned, he also planned to have a quick election, but wimped out at the last minute, denting his reputation in the process. Brown was one of the unluckiest prime ministers: a large black rock has just hit him on the head – this is the Northern Rock crisis, where a bank collapsed and the economy tottered. Now there's a huge oil barrel spiralling through the air – this symbolizes the increasing oil prices, fanning consumer discontent. And did you feel that? The whole building just shook – that's the housing price crash.

Brilliant. We've added the first few dabs of colour to the story of the British prime ministers. The thing to do now is go out and discover a few extra facts about one of these PMs and to try to insert images for these facts into the narrative. You'll soon find that it's a very natural, creative way to learn, well, as much as you want to. Good luck!

PRIME MINISTERS OF GREAT BRITAIN

Robert Walpole
Spencer Compton
Henry Pelham
Duke of Newcastle
Duke of Devonshire
Duke of Newcastle
John Stuart
George Grenville
Marquess of Rockingham
William Pitt the Elder
Duke of Grafton
Lord North
Marquess of Rockingham
William, Earl of Shelburne
William, Duke of Portland
William Pitt the Younger
Henry Addington
William Pitt the Younger
William Grenville
William, Duke of Portland
Spencer Perceval
Earl of Liverpool
George Canning
Viscount Goderich
Duke of Wellington
Earl Grey
William Lamb,
    Viscount Melbourne
Robert 'Bobby' Peel
William Lamb,
    Viscount Melbourne
Lord John Russell
Robert 'Bobby' Peel
Earl of Derby
Earl of Aberdeen
Viscount Palmerston
Earl of Derby
Viscount Palmerston

Lord John Russell
Earl of Derby
Benjamin Disraeli
William Gladstone
Benjamin Disraeli
William Gladstone
Marquess of Salisbury
William Gladstone
Marquess of Salisbury
Earl of Rosebery
Marquess of Salisbury
Arthur Balfour
Henry Campbell-Bannerman
Herbert Asquith
David Lloyd George
Andrew Bonar Law
Stanley Baldwin
James Ramsay Macdonald
Stanley Baldwin
James Ramsay Macdonald
Stanley Baldwin
Neville Chamberlain
Winston Churchill
Winston Churchill
Clement Attlee
Winston Churchill
Anthony Eden
Harold Macmillan
Alec Douglas-Home
Harold Wilson
Edward Heath
Harold Wilson
James Callaghan
Margaret Thatcher
John Major
Tony Blair
Gordon Brown

COUNTRIES OF EUROPE

People are often bewildered by the map of Europe. They ask themselves 'Why so many countries?' and 'Why such silly shapes?'

They may go on to wonder who drew the map, questioning whether he was blind, drunk or just really annoying. Some of them even try to guess whether he had any friends, before shaking their heads with a sigh.

But if you, too, think the map of Europe is a bit of a mess, you need to have another look.

For hidden in among all those lines is a picture – a picture of what happened when an eagle pecked a pentagon.

You may never have considered it before, but the map of Europe tells the story of how, once upon a time, an eagle was quietly sitting with his beer when a pentagon jumped uninvited upon his glass and began to dance around cheekily.

Very naturally, the eagle pecked the pentagon.

That turned out to be the mother of all mistakes. Well, as you can imagine, a huge fight began, with the pentagon calling on its many violent friends for support: a bison, Kermit the frog, a rabbit . . . and the extraordinary pile-up that ensued contains an unforgettable map of Europe.

But I should start at the beginning and tell you the whole story. And, since the eagle is the hero of the tale, we'll begin with him.

Here he is, standing on his perch, spreading his magnificent wings. Let's see what countries he's made of . . .

Look at his head first, which is actually **Switzerland**. The thing about eagles is that, with their amazingly versatile and

well-built beaks, they tend to think of their heads as Swiss-army knifes. That's part of the reason why the eagle will be so quick to peck later on in the story.

At the moment, though, the head looks very neutral, doesn't it? It even has a Swiss flag painted on the beak. This eagle's head is definitely Switzerland.

If you look now to the neck and upper breast of this bird, you'll see that they are covered in the most unusual plumage – these feathers don't belong to an eagle; they're much too long and fluffy. They're the feathers of an ostrich. The neck and breast of the eagle, covered as they are in ostrich feathers, make up **Austria**.

So the neck and breast region is Austria and the head, Switzerland.

And see how, below the breast, the rest of the bird's trunk divides into two, into back and stomach.

It's a lovely back, that. I call it 'Slovak' for short. Slovakians are actually famous for having the most beautiful backs of any European people – soft, smooth and unblemished. This here Slovakian back doesn't let the side down; note the supremely elegant spinal curve, all the way to the bottom of the bird, marking out **Slovakia**.

Exactly beneath Slovakia is the lower part of the eagle's trunk, its stomach. Cor! Listen to it rumble! There's no other bird whose stomach can thunder like this!

It's rumbling so thunderously because the eagle is hungry. And we can mark out the eagle's hungry stomach as **Hungary** on our map. This hungry Hungarian belly runs eastwards parallel to the back.

Now take note of what remains of the bird as we carry on east: its magnificent Romanian tail feathers. Can you see the many Roman emperors' faces that have been printed into these tail feathers? This bird's had Rome-mania ever since he saw the film *Gladiator*.

These Roman remains on the bird are **Romania**, attaching

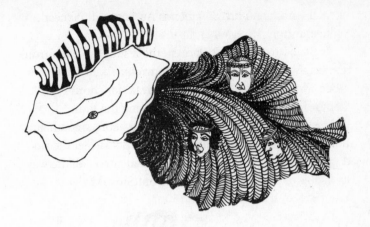

to the hungry part of the bird's trunk, its tummy.

Let's examine the rest of the eagle, beginning with the legs and what it's standing on.

And what legs it has! They're as compact and powerful as you'd ever wish a bird's legs to be: they are utterly superbian. They are Serbian, you see, these legs, which, as is

normal with birds, run down from the stomach. **Serbia** thus protrudes from Hungary and runs bravely south.

At the bottom of these superb Serbian legs the bird's feet and claws, meanwhile, are covered in some kind of yellow gloop. These Macedonian claws seem to have a mass of mustard on them.

Having mustard on your person is something of a tradition in **Macedonia** – the most famous Macedonian, Alexander the Great, sent bags of mustard seed to kings whose armies he'd massacred 'so that they could taste the bitterness of their defeat'. Charming.

On what are these massively mustardy Macedonian feet perching? That's our next question. The answer is that they perch on **Greece**, like the rest of Western civilization.

Greece, an anteater sitting on a rock, is doubled up under the weight of the eagle above him. The eagle, for his part, has to cling on hard – this particular anteater exists on a fast-food diet of deep-fried ants, and is terribly slippery, literally seeping grease from his pores.

Just look at his hands – they're so greasy that all these islands he's been hoarding in his hands over the years are slipping out, tumbling downwards!

Don't forget: this anteater and the islands slipping from its hands make up Greece.

So, our Swiss-headed, Austrian-necked, Slovakian-backed and Hungary-stomached bird is standing with its superb Serbian legs and mustard-covered Macedonian feet upon Greece. Its remains (its Roman-decorated tail-feathering, that is) spread out east and are called Romania.

OK, so we've seen the body of our bird and its perch, but we're yet to take a look at its wings. We'd better head over to them – they're absolutely key to the way the eagle will attack the pentagon later on in our story.

To understand how the eagle's wings work, we need, of course, to consider its shoulders.

They're fantastically strong, as you can see, but the amazing thing about them is the way they thrust at once up and forward from its back, like those of a butterfly swimmer mid-stroke.

This thrusting forward of the shoulder gives the rest of its wing room to move. It's the part of the bird you'd check first if you were testing it for sky-worthiness – that's how vital it is. And, as if we didn't know already that this shoulder is the **Czech Republic**, see how its feathers make a lovely chequered pattern.

The wing itself attaches to this shoulder and runs backwards along the lovely Slovakian back.

It has two main sections: the central area, where the *po*-wer comes from, and the extended tip, which stores the energy and maintains control.

The central, principal area, coming up off the chequered Czech Republic and that lovely Slovakian back, has a beautiful shimmer, doesn't it! It's a pleasure to see such well-polished feathers. This, the power-centre of the wing with its polished feathering, is **Poland**.

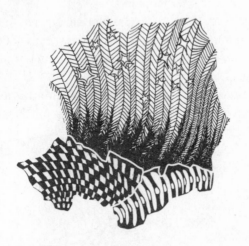

Emerging from the polished Polish portion the magnificent tip heads up and east. Let's look at how this tip energizes and controls the whole wing.

The energy's stored in a set of lithium batteries, which feed straight into powerful, polished Poland. These *lithium* batteries make up **Lithuania**. It's worth noting how the tip of the left-most battery, the one on the leading edge of the wing, has become a little rusty: this is a little bit of Russia in the middle of Europe, rusting away at the end of the foremost lithium Lithuanian battery.

Above Lithuania, there's the Latvian portion of the wing. The feathers on **Latvia** run laterally – which is very important for the aerodynamics. This lateral feathering allows the bird to veer from side to side if need be. This eagle is capable of a *lot of veer* thanks to its Latvia.

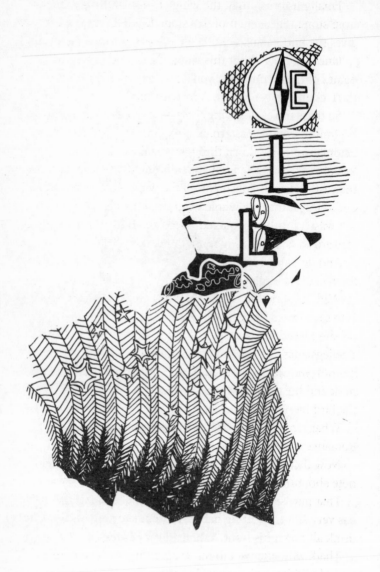

Finally, astonishingly, the wing's E-stonian tip is made from stone. The weight of this stone Estonian tip is what gives the bird balance.

One last thing about this wing: if you read down the names of these countries, you'll see they spell 'ELL', and that the L countries get longer. A mere detail.

So that's the eagle's wing. Let's have one last look at it, beginning from its eastern extreme in stony Estonia. After Estonia, we come down through lateral Latvia (which gives it lots of veer), past the Lithuanian lithium batteries that power the vast, polished Polish part of the wing. And it's important not to forget that the whole wing wouldn't be able to work if it wasn't for the chequered Czech shoulder, throwing itself forward to give the wing room to move.

And, let's just carry on this recap, what do we know about the rest of the eagle?

Well, it's standing on the back of a greasy anteater, which is to say Greece. Its feet, which have masses of mustard on, are Macedonia and its legs (quite superb!) are Serbian. The legs attach to the hungry Hungarian stomach that runs beneath the Slovakian back. Austria is the ostrich-feathered neck and breast into which Slovakia and Hungary feed. And the bird has Switzerland for a head.

What remains? Our eagle's tail feathers of course: Romania.

Now there is, in point of fact, one last thing you should note about this eagle: he's wearing a bib.

That may seem odd, but you have to realize that this eagle has very slovenly eating habits. He tends to slop his food and drink all down his front.

That's why, attached to his Austrian neck and the upper part of his Hungary tummy, he's wearing a bib – to collect the slovenly slop. This bib is Slovenia; it slowly collects spilt food and drink over the course of each day.

So that's the eagle and his bib. Now let's see how this innocent-looking bird found itself in the midst of a punch-up.

Here he is, standing peacefully on his Greek perch, bib at the ready, having a beer. It's all very chilled. He's got a special Iberian mug for his *Iberian* beer: it's in the amusing shape of a Spanish bull's head, and it has a *Portuguese* handle to make it *port*able.

So the handle of the eagle's novelty beer mug, the bit that ensures it's portable, is **Portugal**. And we know that this is a Spanish bull's head because **Spain** is the land of bull-fighting, and only in Spain would anyone think of manufacturing such a mug.

These two countries, Portugal and Spain, constitute the eagle's beery Iberian Peninsula.

BUT LOOK! This is the bit we've all been waiting for! A pentagon, a miniature pentagonal Frenchman, has just leapt up on to the eagle's beer. He's on the rim of the mug now, **France** doing a quite ridiculous dance. What a piece of provocation!

It takes a Frenchman to wiggle his hips so brazenly at an eagle, stopping him from drinking. And it's getting worse. Now he's doing star jumps!

Here we go – this'll serve him right! With a powerful flap of his wings, the eagle has just launched his sharp Swiss beak towards the pentagonal Frenchman and pecked him mightily

in the ribs! Blood spurts out – some of it even slopping into that Slovenian bib.

With a blood-curdling scream, the Frenchman calls for help – and with this cry the fight really begins.

Listen to this! Are your ears beginning to ring with the stampeding sound coming from the east? That's the sound of a charging bison! Most likely, it's one of France's friends . . . the eagle had better brace himself!

Now you may be under the impression that there aren't any bison in Europe. Nonsense. The people of the **Ukraine** have been reintroducing them like billy-o since the sixties. They now have eleven herds.

So you can bet your bottom dollar that this rumbling monster, only yards away now, is one of those Ukrainian bison.

Watch now as the Ukrainian bison, horns lowered, charges at the eagle's vulnerable rear. It's as clear as daylight what he wants to do – he wants to bite this eagle on the bottom, despite the impressive flaring of the bird's Romanian tail feathers protecting its rear.

But what quick thinking from the bison! As quick as a flash he immediately changes course, leaping up and planting his front legs on the tail feathers, using his weight to push them right down into the Serbian legs. He's in!

Almost perfect. The only thing is that with this sudden jump he's accidentally kicked up a mouldy black fish from behind the bird and now has to mould himself over this thing, which is trapped between his front legs and Romania. This mouldy black fish he's trying to mould himself over is **Moldova**, sandwiched now between Romania and the Ukraine.

And this means his head is still well short of the target. He'll have to crane his neck forward (what flexibility he has!) if he wants any chance of biting the eagle's bottom . . .

'AWWWW!' cries the bird, the noise muffled because his beak is still deep in the Frenchman.

That looks unbelievably painful! Our bison has hit his target so exactly that his teeth have sunk into both the top and bottom halves of the bird. Blood is spewing from the ends of both the Slovakian back and the hungry Hungarian stomach!

What a remarkable attack! And, as if this weren't enough, his horns are driving into the lower half of the bird's polished Polish wing.

So with this onslaught the Ukraine has managed to border Romania, Hungary, Slovakia and Poland – as well as moulding the mouldy fish of Moldova into Romania.

You'd think that this would cause the eagle to give up pecking the French pentagon, eh?

Surprisingly, though, he doesn't seem especially fazed by what's happened. He's still sturdily standing there gnawing at the Frenchman. There's only one outward sign of stress: a very subtle drooping in his outstretched wing.

Now, since the eagle is being rather ganged up upon here, I hope you don't mind if I help steady him a little.

Look – there's a bell here, and it can be put to good use. If we place it up on the bison's back, and force it tight against the wing, it'll keep the polished, the lithium and the lateral portions in place.

There we go! We couldn't hope for a better fit . . .

This ruse with the bell we'll call **Belarus**. I think we can agree that the eagle won't have any more problems with drooping wings!

And just in time too. Some more of whimpering France's friends are ganging up to attack our eagle . . .

There are two of them and they're acting as a pair – which is no surprise: they were allies in the last war, they both excel at football and they adore terrible pop music. It's **Italy** and **Germany** that we can see plotting their attack. Let's have a good look at them.

Germany has disguised himself as the head of Kermit the frog – he's calling himself Kermany. Huh!

He's amusing himself (and us, to be fair) with a remarkable trick: he's bouncing a Danish pastry up and down on his head like it's a football. He's showing great concentration and control – and no wonder: he's German. His partner is Italy, which (you may know) resembles a boot.

And what a beautiful boot this is – it's Versace, made from the finest Italian leather.

The Italian boot and Kermit's German head have prepared a pincer movement; they last did this in WWII. Unlike then, though, their aim here is to asphyxiate an eagle.

In they come now! Fingers crossed for the bird!

The Italian boot leads the attack, coming in first, from below. Here it is, powering in against the head and neck with a mighty push. BOOM! It forces the bib and France's foot right out of the way to throttle the bird's throat, which emits an awful sound, like it's been hit by a boot in the head and neck. A sort of mournful 'caaaaaaaw'.

If Austria and Switzerland think this is bad they'd better steel themselves for worse, for here comes Kermany, powering in between France and Poland!

Oops! He's just smacked painfully into the top of France, bouncing off with a clunk! A tighter space than he'd expected, obviously. He's judged that one terribly.

But he's coming in for another go now and this time he gets it perfectly. He's come down like a ton of bricks exactly where he needed to: on the head and neck of the bird. Pincer movements don't come any better than this double whammy from Germany and Italy – the poor eagle will do well to survive.

I mean, you just have to look at what Kermany, especially, has just achieved and take your hat off to his bravery!

To get himself into the space, he's had to suffer all sorts. With France against the back of his head, a load of Polish polish in his eye and Switzerland and Italy tight beneath his neck, he's also had to endure the bird's chequered shoulder, the Czech Republic, in his mouth.

And you know the most impressive thing of all? Kermany's managed to do all this while bouncing a Danish pastry on his head. **Denmark**, the country this pastry represents, is now balanced perfectly atop Kermany's Germany.

As a result of this heroism, though, the poor eagle's begun to let out a desperate, choking whine. Things are really beginning to go against him.

At least he'll find a whiff of consolation in knowing he's not the only one in pain. During the pincer movement, you see, France received that awful bang on the head from Kermany.

As a result, France's head is beginning to bulge. The bulge is Belgium, and it's expanding before our eyes . . . By golly, look at this! It has puffed up like a miniature airbag so fast that it's actually trapping a luckless bird, **Luxembourg**, in the nook between the pentagon and Kermit. Luckless bird Luxembourg will remain trapped here for ever.

The only way to soothe a bang to the head this violent is of course to slather the injury with hollandaise sauce. So that's what we'll do to soothe bulging **Belgium**.

An all round master cure, hollandaise sauce is without compare. There's not an ailment to any part of the body it can't soothe. It *never lands* in the wrong place so far as the patient is concerned. Perhaps this is why Holland is part of the **Netherlands**.

If we just pour the gloopy hollandaise into the V this bulge now makes with the back of German Kermit's head, then that'll keep the pain and swelling down nicely with the perfect poultice that we'll call the Netherlands. There we go! No need to carry on complaining now, France.

So this has turned into something of a fight, eh? What have we got so far?

Well, we've got pentagonal France (with a now bulging head) on the rim of an Iberian beer (the Spanish mug with the Portuguese handle). We've got a flapping, bibbed eagle, standing on Greece, pecking this pentagon. There's a bison standing on the eagle's Romanian tail feathers, successfully biting the bird's bottom and ruffling its polished wing with his horns. There's a bell from Belarus too – we placed it in there to support the wing tip. And we've just had a pincer movement from Kermit's German head (plus Danish pastry) and an Italian boot – a move that is cutting the air off from our poor eagle's throat.

Run over these elements in your mind for a second to make sure they're all in place.

Returning to the scene, it looks like the eagle is just about hanging on in there. He's shaking at the knees a little, to be sure, but he'll not admit defeat just yet.

With so little oxygen now reaching those superb Serbian legs, it's hard to imagine how he'll be able to cope with another attack.

And that's bad news for him, because, look at this, yet another of France's friends has piled in to join the fray.

Oh! It's a bunny rabbit – not so scary! He'll get himself hurt, won't he?

Maybe, in fact, he won't . . . Look, the wily fur ball is staying out of harm's way, doing what he does best in the evening: snoozing.

He's sprung up now on top of this European pile-up and is reclining for a comfortable nap!

You've got to give him this: he's *ball*sy. He is, in fact, the *Baltic* Sea.

Look how carefully he's arranging himself! He has planted his bottom on the top of the polished Polish wing, stretched his toes to the Danish pastry and, with his ears pointing high into the air, he's using the wing tip as a back-rest.

Best of all – this really is worth savouring – look how he's suavely slotted his elbow right over Estonia.

What a performance from our ballsy Baltic rabbit!

Yes, it looks casual, but this rabbit may well be the straw that breaks the camel's back: the eagle's legs are beginning to give way; he's buckling at the knee!

Dear me. We can't just sit here and watch this! Quick – we have to help. It's about ten against one in there!

It's obvious what we've got to do. We'll have to bulk up those legs of his and strengthen the Balkans, which is the whole area around his Serbian legs.

The fact is, if the eagle can stay on his feet, he'll probably survive.

Well, what do we have to hand? What can we use to support him? Come on – anything will help! Grab whatever's there . . .

A box of Albanian Alpen. Great.

An abandoned Bulgarian burglar's sack with loads of stolen loot tumbling out? All right. Anything else?

A bottle of knee-growing cream belonging to a man named Monty? Unlikely to help, but maybe we'll put it to some good use.

A crocodile's head with mobile jaws? Every little helps.

Even these here Bosnian parsnips you've now given me, I suppose.

Is that all the objects we have? OK, then. We'll have to make the most of this motley collection, eh?

Now how, exactly, are we going to do this?

Well, our bedrock is inevitably Greece, so we can begin there.

First things first: let's shore up the back of the legs where there is a big gap between Greece and the beleaguered Romanian tail feathers. What would fit in there?

I know, that bulging sack of burglar's loot should do

the job. Come on! Wedge it in . . . there she goes! Between Greece and Romania, this area that's now bulging with a burglar's sack, lies **Bulgaria**.

Now for the front of the bird, to the west of the superbian legs.

Again, we'll build up from the bedrock of Greece.

First, we can lay the Albanian Alpen tight against the eagle's massively mustardy Macedonian claws and its superb Serbian shins. This sturdy Albanian cereal will stand on Greece and border Macedonia, the feet and shin sections of the Serbia legs.

On top of the Alpen, we'll place our man Monty's bottle of knee-growing cream (**Montenegro** for short). We'll position

it with the nozzle open against the Serbian knee in the hope that the balm will seep out and strengthen the bone there. Superb though his knee-bones already are, they need all the help they can get.

So Montenegro sits atop **Albania**, and against the very middle of the Serbian leg.

What we have to do now is our biggest engineering challenge: we have to bridge the gap from here all the way up to the bib, and thereby support the chest. If we can do that, then our eagle will be as sturdy as you like and stand every chance of surviving this fight.

Out of this croc's crunching jaws and these parsnips, we need to fashion a solid block that will fit the gap.

Our problem is, the croc's jaws (which stand for **Croatia**, by the way) have a tendency to keep swinging open and shut, we really need them to be a bit more solid, wouldn't you say?

Aha! I've got it! We'll stuff the Bosnian parsnips into its jaws, wedging them open . . .

Well done, that's come off beautifully; no amount of force will be able to get this croc to close its mouth!

Incidentally, the parsnips doing the filling are Bosnian, as

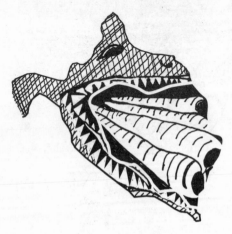

you may have guessed, because if you have a parsnip in your mouth and attempt to name it, the sound that comes out is 'Bosnia'. You can try this at home.

Amusing fact: Arnold Schwarzenegger, Governor of California, used to own these Bosnian parsnips, but he cut his lip on one, and threw them all away. 'You Bosnians,' he said, 'hurt zee governor – that is vy I srow you avay'. These Bosnian Parsnips that once hurt the governor are the country known in full as **Bosnia and Herzegovina**.

OK, all that now remains is to wedge the Croatian croc's jaws and Bosnian bundle into the gap between Montenegro and Serbia.

To do so, we'll hook the sharp fangs of the upper jaw into the eagle's upper thigh, and its lower jaw's fangs into the bottle of knee-grow, and with one last parsnip to really tighten the whole thing up, we have a result . . . a seamless structural support. Take a look at our handiwork now!

So, this is good. We've ended up supporting our eagle with a burglar's bulging sack (Bulgaria, at the back); and with a box of Albanian Alpen, a bottle of Monty's knee-grow cream (Montenegro), some Bosnian parsnips and a Croatian crocodile's jaw.

We can all relax. The pile-up, once dangerously unstable, has become so safely balanced that no one's capable of budging an inch. From terrible violence, all of a sudden, we have a pretty harmonious scene. Or, at least, stalemate. How gratifying!

It is this scene of apparent harmony and peace that greets the eyes of a gorgeous mermaid who now walks in. Don't worry, she's no friend of the Frenchman; she's not come to assist him. She has been out all day picking swedes in the nearby fields and knows nothing of the fight.

Indeed, the sight of this sturdy pile of objects and animals looks warm and snug to her tired eyes and exhausted fins – it makes her think of bed. So much so, indeed, that she decides to climb on top and sleep there for the night.

So this beautiful mermaid (who's covered in shimmering fins – she's a Finnish mermaid) begins to arrange herself for sleep.

Kneeling on the rabbit's casually extended arm (the one weighing suavely upon the wing tip of Estonia), she leans herself sleepily forward against the warm fur of his long ears, curling her elegant tail beneath her. Then, once she has perched her ample bosom on top of these ears, she slings her sack of swedes over the rabbit's front.

Although very endearing, you have to say that this is pretty scandalous behaviour!

We must be in Scandinavia near **Finland** and **Sweden**. Considering the mermaid is Finnish and has a Swedish sack of swedes, there can really be no doubt of that.

The final thing that our Finnish mermaid does before

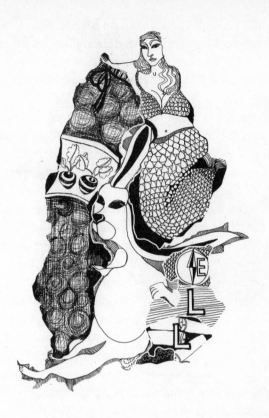

falling asleep is to drape a cosy Norwegian blanket right over herself, making sure that it covers the swedes too. Northern **Norway** covers Scandinavia completely, and how snug everyone looks, sealed away from the cold!

And that's just about it – this Norwegian blanket is the icing on the proverbial cake! The map is complete.

And to think all this happened just because a Frenchman danced on an eagle's beer!

My only sadness in all of this is that Euro-sceptic **Britain and Ireland**, refused to get involved – it would have been interesting to see how they would have influenced the fight. You can actually see them, hovering away above France,

remaining stoically uninterested in the whole thing.

Anyhow, well done for getting this far. Just to make sure you've absorbed this touching tale, let's just run through, one last time, the story of how an eagle pecked at a pentagon and triggered an almighty free-for-all.

Well. The eagle was quietly standing on a greasy anteater, Greece, wasn't he, when it all kicked off. His feet had masses of mustard on, they were Macedonia, and were attached, as you would expect, to his superb Serbian legs. They ran up into his hungry Hungarian tummy, which had the Slovakian back on top, of course. The breast, uniting back and stomach, was covered in the ostrich feathers of Austria, while the pecking head was obviously Swiss.

The eagle's enormous chequered shoulder, thrown
forward from the Slovakian back, was rippling with muscle
beneath the chequered feathers of the Czech Republic. The
wing (rising up off the shoulder and back) was gleaming,
wasn't it, with Polish polish. Above Poland were the
Lithuanian lithium batteries (the leading one's tip rusty and
Russian); above them, the lateral feathers of Latvia leading
up to the astonishing and stony eastern wing tip of Estonia.

Reading downwards, these countries names went 'ELL'
and the Ls got longer: Estonia, Latvia, Lithuania. All these sit
high above the Romanian tail feathers.

So that was the bird, and he was wearing his slovenly
Slovenian bib as he quietly drank from his Iberian beer, a

Spanish bull's head made portable by its Portuguese handle. But at that point the pentagonal Frenchman of France hopped on to the rim and began to lark about. He got pecked, of course, by the eagle's Swiss beak.

Then all hell broke loose: a thundering Ukrainian bison came first, forcing a mouldy black fish up against the Romanian tail feathers as he trod on them to bite the bird's butt (while horning its polished wing). That mouldy fish he had to mould himself over was Moldova.

This was the point of our first intervention, the moment where we waded in on the side of the bird, putting a bell on the bison's back to support the eagle's wing tip. Remember? That was Belarus.

But the eagle's predicament soon worsened again when German Kermit (or Kermany, as he calls himself) and Italian boot came in together and clamped his head and neck in a fearsomely well co-ordinated pincer manoeuvre, all the more impressive for Kermit's balancing a Danish pastry on his head throughout the whole operation. And it didn't fall off, even when, on the first attack, Kermit knocked into France by accident, causing it a bulging bump called Belgium.

That Belgian bulge, of course, trapped the luckless bird of Luxembourg between France and Germany, but we tried to treat the swelling with the hollandaise sauce of the Netherlands.

At this point, with the eagle already straining under the pressure, the arrival of our ballsy Baltic rabbit tipped the balance. He swanned in to put his knees up over the Danish pastry, sitting on top of the polished wing and leaning back on the three-part E-L-L wing tip. Things were now so unfair that we just *had* to intervene again – especially with the eagle beginning to totter.

So we bulked up the bird's legs in the Balkans with a selection of ready-to-hand objects. Behind the knees, as a first move, we shored things up by forcing that bulging burglar's sack tight into the gap between the greasy anteater's back and the bird's tail feathers. That was Bulgaria.

At the front of the legs, building upwards from Greece, we used Albanian Alpen and Monty's knee-growing lotion from Montenegro to support the lower leg. We then made a sturdy block from the unlikely combo of a Croatian crocodile's gaping jaws and some Bosnian parsnips – posnias, that is – that has once 'hurt zee governor' (Bosnia and Herzegovina). The croc's upper teeth dug into the eagle's leg while the lower ones punctured the bottle of knee-grow. Between these two jaws, the Bosnian (and Herzegovinan) parsnips ensured everything was nice and solid.

The whole thing worked beautifully. The fight stopped completely – no one could move at all (with the possible exception of the rabbit, who was too lazy to do so).

The scene was so peaceful, indeed, that a passing Finnish mermaid – Finland – covered in shimmering fins and carrying a bag of swedes, thought she'd kip on top for the night. So she laid her front against the rabbit, slung her bag of swedes (Sweden) over the top and covered the pile with a snug Norwegian blanket.

So that's that, then. Heartiest congratulations on reaching the end. By asking yourself a few questions and finding the answers in your imagination, you'll soon perfect your knowledge of the whereabouts, shapes and borders of all the European nations.

As ever, my advice is to turn your new knowledge, after a little more practice, to financial gain.

Greece
Macedonia
Serbia
Hungary
Slovakia
Austria
Switzerland
Czech Republic
Poland
Estonia
Latvia
Lithuania
Slovenia
Spain
Portugal
France
Ukraine
Romania

Moldova
Belarus
Germany
Italy
Denmark
Belgium
Netherlands
Bulgaria
Albania
Montenegro
Croatia
Bosnia and
    Herzegovina
Finland
Sweden
Norway
Great Britain
    and Ireland

ACKNOWLEDGEMENTS

I would like to acknowledge those who have helped me in writing this book.

Above all, my thanks go to my mother and father, for countless reasons. Perhaps the least of them is that it was they who coerced me, one Sunday afternoon, into reading aloud a very early draft of the book to the whole family, along with various of my sisters' friends and love-interests then stalking the kitchen. I'd like to thank all those present for the flood of helpful suggestions, not to mention ribald abuse, that peppered that reading. It had a profound effect on many aspects of the book and, indeed, on the very methods used to write it. Chief among these was the decision that all mnemonics within the book be repeatedly and rigorously tested on anyone kind enough to listen.

This experimental technique has, I am aware, been a source of great suffering for friends and colleagues. First in the firing line have been those at home. Henrietta Williams and Barbara Pizl deserve a lifetime's supply of orchids, at the least, for their sunny tolerance and help, while Daithi Roche has earned the cognomen 'top-dog' many times over. Similarly, I owe deep thanks to my employers at Inspire-education, Neil and Stew Denley; to Dickon Ausden, Mel Riggall, Katy Band, Alastair Scott-Dalgleish, Karl Knoll, Juliette Danjon, Erica Jarnes, George Horton and L'Equipe.

It is a pleasure to acknowledge the role played by my polymath chauffeur, Dan James, in the writing of this book. Much of the work was done peripatetically, you see, as work took me round the schools of the Midlands. Dan, between jobs, kindly responded to a friend in need and drove me about. So acute were his many suggestions, so patient, helpful and creative his advice, that our author–chauffeur roles were at times in danger of being reversed. It was nonetheless a constant boon to my morale to know not only that I had a driver, but that he had just scored a top-40 single.

Various members of the Askesian Society have read proofs of this work and commented helpfully: particularly Al Hearn, Adrian De Froment, Hamid Khanbhai, Jonny Lowndes and Paul Reeve. They have my warmest thanks and friendship. As do four teachers, for assorted guidance and inspiration: Colin Fraser, Kevin O'Regan, Kia Nobre and John Sutton.

Not least for her indulgence, I'd like to thank my mus-ical dance partner, Orlanda Ward; I'm also indebted to my grandmother for consultancy on family history. Many ideas, and much fun, has meanwhile come from and through teaching – thanks in particular to Josh and Dinah Foer, Jamie Onslow and the citizens of Wem; and, of course, to all those who have turned out on foggy Sunday mornings for the original memory walks that were the book's inspiration.

This book would never have been written were it not for the 'memory championships community', who serve as a kind of amateur research programme in ways to enhance human memory and are a constant source of insight and camaraderie. Thanks to all, but notably Dominic O'Brien, who first introduced me to memory techniques, and my mentor and training-partner, Lukas Amsuess.

It is with an emotion bordering on sadness that I express my thanks to Yeti McCaldin, who has done such wonders with the illustrations. The thought that she will not always be at hand to depict my thoughts is a stinger; it has been a pleasure working with her.

Lastly, and most of all, it is with immense gratitude and respect that I acknowledge and express my thanks to my gifted and skilful editor, Jenny Dean. She shaped this book from its very inception and her gaiety, focus and taste have sustained my efforts, and much improved them.